David Edgar

David Edgar was born into a theatre family and took up writing full time in 1972. In 1989, he founded Britain's first graduate playwriting course, at the University of Birmingham, of which he was director for ten years. He was appointed as Britain's first Professor of Playwriting in 1995.

His stage adaptations include Albie Sachs' *Jail Diary*, Charles Dickens's *Nicholas Nickleby* (both for the Royal Shakespeare Company), Gitta Sereny's biography of *Albert Speer* (for the National Theatre) and Julian Barnes's *Arthur & George* (for Birmingham Rep and Nottingham Playhouse). He has written two community plays for Dorchester: *Entertaining Strangers* and *A Time to Keep* (with Stephanie Dale). His original plays for the RSC include *Destiny*, *Maydays* and *Pentecost*, the second in a series of plays about Eastern Europe after the Cold War, following *The Shape of the Table* (National Theatre) and preceding *The Prisoner's Dilemma* (RSC). His most recent plays are *Written on the Heart* (RSC), *Playing with Fire* (National Theatre) and *Testing the Echo* (Out of Joint).

David Edgar's television work includes the three-part BBC2 serial *Vote for Them* (written with Neil Grant) and *Buying a Landslide* (also for BBC2). He wrote the film *Lady Jane* for Paramount. His recent radio work includes an adaptation of Eve Brook's novel *The Secret Parts* and *Something wrong about the mouth*, both for BBC Radio 4.

He is President of the Writers' Guild.

How Plays Work

David Edgar

NICK HERN BOOKS
London
www.nickhernbooks.co.uk

A Nick Hern Book

How Plays Work
first published in Great Britain in 2009
as a paperback original by Nick Hern Books Limited,
The Glasshouse, 49a Goldhawk Road, London W12 8QP

Reprinted 2009, 2010 (twice), 2011, 2012

Cover designed by www.energydesignstudio.com

Typeset by Nick Hern Books, London
Printed and bound in Great Britain by
CPI Antony Rowe, Chippenham, Wiltshire

A CIP catalogue record for this book
is available from the British Library

ISBN 978 1 85459 371 9

To Amy, Tim and Lucy Downing

Contents

Acknowledgements

The author and publisher gratefully acknowledge permission to quote from the following:

A Chorus of Disapproval by Alan Ayckbourn (© 1986), *The Entertainer* by John Osborne (© 1961), and *Plenty* by David Hare (© 1978), all published by Faber and Faber Ltd.

Cigarettes and Chocolate by Anthony Minghella, published in *Best Radio Plays of 1988* (© 1989), *The Cripple of Inishmaan* by Martin McDonagh (© 1997), *Epsom Downs* by Howard Brenton (© 1977), *Lear* by Edward Bond (© 1972, 1978), *Top Girls* by Caryl Churchill (© 1982, 1984, 1990, 1991), and *Shopping and Fucking* by Mark Ravenhill (© 1996, 1997), all published by Methuen Drama, an imprint of A&C Black Publishers Ltd.

Icecream by Caryl Churchill (© 1989), *My Night with Reg* by Kevin Elyot (© 1994), and *The Winslow Boy* by Terence Rattigan (© 1953), all published by Nick Hern Books Ltd.

Grace by Sarah Woods (© 2003), published by Oberon Modern Plays.

Classical Literary Criticism, translated by T.S. Dorsch (© 1965), published by Penguin Classics.

Writing in Restaurants by David Mamet (© 1986), published by Viking Penguin, a division of Penguin Group (USA) Inc.

Bouncers by John Godber (© 1987), first published by and reproduced with the permission of Josef Weinberger Ltd (English Theatre Guild Ltd).

Our Friends in the North by Peter Flannery (Broadcast on BBC2 in 1996).

Every effort has been made to contact copyright holders. The publishers will be glad to make good in any future editions any errors or omissions brought to their attention.

Preface:
Beginnings

First things first. You know all this already.

This book is about mechanisms and techniques which are familiar to us as audiences, because they work on us whenever we watch a play or a television drama or a film. What I've tried to do is to name and describe those techniques, to position them in categories, and to gather them together into a theory. In *A Midsummer Night's Dream*, Theseus speaks of 'the poet's eye, in a fine frenzy rolling', which brings forth things unknown, turns them to shapes, and gives them 'a local habitation and a name'. I hope there's a bit of fine frenzy in this book, but its basic purpose is the placing of parts, and the naming of names.

Although intended to be useful to anyone interested in plays and how they work, this book started out as a series of workshops for playwrights. In the mid-1970s, I ran a fortnightly playwriting option at the University of Birmingham for undergraduate drama students (fortunately for me, they included Terry Johnson and Louise Page). It was clear from this experience that there were ways of thinking about dramatic problems (on the level of where scenes start and end, who's on the stage and how to get them on and off) which can be collectively explored and individually applied. In the late 1980s, the then head of the Birmingham department, Gerry McCarthy, asked me to consider designing and running a postgraduate course, to extend and develop the work I'd done at undergraduate level.

Although located in a university, I saw Birmingham's MA (now M.Phil) in Playwriting Studies as an outgrowth of a self-help movement among playwrights that had taken off earlier in the decade, in response to a questioning of the quality of new plays by critics and, increasingly, directors. The most prominent self-help group was the Manchester-based North-West Playwrights, founded in Manchester in 1982 by the local branch of the Theatre Writers' Union; there were also groups in the North East and, later, the West Midlands. Three of the underlying principles of the Birmingham course, then and now – that it is taught by practising playwrights, that it combines theoretical exploration with work on student texts, and that it involves live performance of students' work – were principles that defined the self-help movement.

It was also based on the notion that there was something to learn. The playwright Howard Brenton once pointed out that the stage play is as tight a form as the eighteenth-century sonata. It lasts between two and three hours (usually), is performed in two or three chunks (typically), and consists of a group of people almost always in one place presenting an enacted story to another group of people sitting in front of or sometimes around them. It's not surprising that an art form squeezed into such narrow confines has built up a repertoire of conventions which its audiences bring with them into the playhouse whether theatre-makers like it or not, and which aspirant playwrights can study.

When the course began in the autumn of 1989, we quickly discovered that this is not a universally accepted truth. In our second year, I wrote a piece about new writing in *The Independent*,[1] which provoked a distinguished British playwright to claim that the real problem with contemporary drama was the existence of my course. From the beginning, we were up against the British cult of the crusty amateur: that prejudice which, in the theatre, is expressed in the belief that while actors can benefit from training (along with stage managers and other footsoldiers of the craft), directors and writers are supposed to aquire their skills telepathically; that the very idea of training devalues the status and may indeed stunt the imagination of the lone artist engaged in isolated struggle with the muse.

From the start, the course was divided into exploration of the students' own work (which happened on Mondays) and study of the contemporary and historical canon (on Tuesdays). The idea was that theatre writing is both an art and a craft, a distinction which could also be expressed as first draft versus second draft, play-writing versus playwrighting, getting it good versus getting it right. Monday and Tuesday thinking became a shorthand; Stephen Lowe's and later Richard Pinner's Monday workshops were about fine frenzy, releasing the imagination, letting inspiration take you where it will. While Tuesdays were about creating order out of chaos, cleaning up, fixing, licking into shape. Of course, in reality, these two approaches overlapped. As we insisted, not everybody writes their first and second drafts that way. But everybody has to work through both processes at some point or another.

In early 1996, I spent three months as a Judith E. Wilson Visiting Fellow at Clare Hall, Cambridge, during which the contents of the early Tuesday seminars expanded into what I grandly called a foundation course, which I taught at the start of the MA year, and which is the basis of what follows. Initially, these sessions had been structured around a narrowing focus: I began by looking at the building blocks of whole plays, then the elements of scenes, and finally a menu of devices. At Cambridge, I added sections on character, play structure and genre, and confirmed my growing conviction that all these components share a fundamental dramatic shape, the argument with which I conclude this book.

In its development, I am hugely indebted to the writers and directors who came to Birmingham to talk about the plays and playwrights they admired. Much of what I say about Chekhov is gleaned from Trevor Griffiths's sessions on *The Cherry Orchard* and Max Stafford-Clark's on *Three Sisters*. Howard Brenton deepened my understanding of Brecht in his seminar on the telescope scene in *The Life of Galileo*, and Stephen Jeffreys found a way of saying most of what needs saying about writing large scenes in his study of the park scene in *The Man of Mode*. I remember a Birmingham-to-London train journey during which Joe Penhall gave an impromptu, personal tutorial on the difference between two-handers and three-handers; screenwriter Michael Eaton introduced me to the concept of liminality; my conversations with April de Angelis led to my asking her to take over the course when I retired in 1999 (which she duly did). In our first year, Anthony Minghella outlined ten basic principles of playwriting which I have plundered mercilessly ever since.

Most of all, I learnt from the 115 students who did the MA during my time at Birmingham University, who included my later successors Sarah Woods and Steve Waters. Another course graduate – the playwright Stephanie Dale – has either read or heard all of this book (much of it many times). Without her insight, encouragement and patience, it would not have been written.

Justifying the title

In his preface to *The Modern British Novel*, Malcolm Bradbury admitted that the only incontestable element in his title was the definite article.[2] As a title, *How Plays Work* could appear similarly hubristic. It could mean merely 'how some plays work', or even 'how some of some plays work' or 'how some of some plays work some of the time'. I would defend the book's thesis, but I appreciate that it, too, is bound by its times.

It is certainly based on a limited sample, which is partly about my taste, partly about the taste of my colleagues, and partly about the repertoire of the British theatre when I was growing up (many of the plays cited are those which my parents – who worked and met at the Birmingham Repertory Theatre – took me to or enabled me to see). So, there's a great deal from the British theatrical grand narrative, from Shakespeare via the Restoration, Sheridan and Shaw to the flowering of new drama since the Second World War. There's some classical Greeks, a lot of Ibsen and Chekhov, Brecht and Arthur Miller; but regrettably little from the French, Italian, Spanish or German theatres, at least before 1900. There is little reference to physical, live, devised and/or event theatre, partly because so few of its texts are published or otherwise accessible. To compensate, I have drawn many examples from other dramatic media, from films, television and radio. This is partly because this book started out as a seminar series, and these examples as illustrative clips. But referring to film and television underlines my belief that there is more in common between the dramatic media than is generally acknowledged; or, at the very least, that stage playwrights can learn more from their sister media than they sometimes think. There is also some academic reference, again drawn from a fairly limited range, but here I make less apology. A quick flip through the endnotes will make clear how much I owe to Marvin Carlson's encyclopaedic *Theories of the Theatre*, Eric Bentley's *The Life of the Drama*, J.L. Styan's *The Elements of Drama*, John Lennard and Mary Luckhurst's *The Drama Handbook* and all of Peter Brook's writings on the theatre.

Finally, back to fine frenzies and the distinction between Monday and Tuesday thinking. There is undoubtedly a danger that books like this will encourage mechanical and formalistic writing; the huge mushrooming of playwriting courses and literary departments in theatres over the last twenty years has fanned those fears. In 1788, Friedrich Schiller wrote a letter to a friend whose inspiration had been smothered by his intellect. Schiller's message was, that while the good is ineffective without the right, the right will not exist without the good:

> The ground for your complaint seems to me to lie in the constraint imposed by your reason upon your imagination... It seems a bad thing and detrimental to the creative work of the mind if Reason makes too close an examination of the ideas as they come pouring in – at the very gateway, as it were. Looked at in isolation, a thought may seem very trivial or very fantastic; but it may be made important by another thought that comes after it, and, in conjunction with other thoughts that may seem equally absurd, it may turn out to form a most effective link. Reason cannot form any opinion upon all this unless it retains the thought long enough to look at it in connection with the others. On the other hand, where there is a creative mind, Reason – so it seems to me – relaxes its watch upon the gates, and the ideas rush in pell-mell, and only then does it look them through and examine them in a mass... You complain of your unfruitfulness because you reject too soon and discriminate too severely.[3]

This book argues that playwriting is an activity subject to the constraints of reason. Nonetheless, Schiller's warning is a good place to begin.

1. David Edgar, 'Looking Forward', *The Independent*, 8 May 1991.

2. Malcolm Bradbury, *The Modern British Novel*, London: Secker and Warburg, 1993, p. ix.

3. Quoted in Philip Rieff, *Freud: The Mind of the Moralist*, Chicago: University of Chicago Press, 1979, pp. 88-9.

1
Audiences

Audiences

What am I describing?

1) A town is threatened by a malevolent force of nature. A leading citizen seeks to take the necessary action to protect the town from this danger, but finds that the economic interests of the town are ranged against him and he ends up in battle alone.

2) Two sisters are unjustly preferred over a third sister. Despite their efforts, the younger sister marries into royalty and her wicked sisters are confounded.

3) A young woman is pledged to a young man, but finds that a parent has plans for her to marry someone else. Calling on the assistance of a priest and a nurse, the young couple plot to evade the fate in store for them.

4) A married couple is at war. A younger influence enters their lives, providing a sexual temptation which threatens the marriage. But ultimately, the couple finds that although they find it hard to live together, they cannot live apart.

5) A man who has scaled many heights senses that his powers have deserted him. A woman from his past re-enters his life, and provokes him to take one last, fatal climb.

6) With her father's encouragement, a young woman allows herself to be wooed by a prince. Her brother moves a long way away. The prince behaves increasingly peculiarly and

abusively, and, shortly after the death of the woman's father, leaves on board a ship. The woman goes mad, alarms the Royal Family, gives everybody flowers, escapes from her minders, and dies in a suspicious accident. The brother returns, angry, at the head of a popular army. There is a contest over the funeral arrangements between family, church and state. The prince returns and he and the woman's brother end up fighting over the coffin.

Regular theatre and cinema audiences will recognise some of these summaries, and people who enjoy parlour games might have spotted that all of them describe more than one play, film, or story. The first is the story of *Jaws*, but also Ibsen's *An Enemy of the People*. The second outlines the situation at the beginning of both *King Lear* and *Cinderella*. The first sentence of the third summary is the action of most comedies written between the fifth century BC and the end of the nineteenth century; with the second sentence, it describes *Romeo and Juliet*, and the subplot of John Vanbrugh's *The Relapse*. In Oscar Wilde's *The Importance of Being Earnest*, both Jack and Algernon seek to fulfil their romantic ambitions with the aid of a priest and a governess.

The fourth description applies to a host of nineteenth- and twentieth-century marriage plays: obviously to August Strindberg's *The Dance of Death* and Edward Albee's *Who's Afraid of Virginia Woolf?*; but also to Noël Coward's *Private Lives*, John Osborne's *Look Back in Anger* and Peter Nichols' *Passion Play*. The fifth outlines the common action of three of Ibsen's last four plays (*The Master Builder*, *John Gabriel Borkman* and *When We Dead Awaken*), in all of which old men are confronted by women from their past, and end up climbing towers or mountains, to their doom.

On the last one, I'm not the first to spot the parallels between the tragedy of Hamlet and that of Diana, Princess of Wales.

There is a danger of taking this idea too far. In the mid-'50s, London audiences probably didn't notice that two groundbreaking new plays both had five characters and one set, and included long speeches, a crucial offstage character, music-hall turns, people taking off their trousers, elements of the first half being echoed in the second, nothing much happening, and the two protagonists spending the play trying to leave and ending up agreeing to stay. The reason why playgoers are unlikely to have spotted these similiarities between *Waiting for Godot* and *Look Back in Anger* is because they employ completely opposite strategies to represent the conditions of their time.

Nonetheless, audiences do recognise that plays, which are on the surface as different as can be, can share an underlying architecture. I'm aware how unpopular this idea is for playwrights beginning their careers. Properly, playwrights insist that their voice is unique, and they don't want to start a new project with an audit of how many other people have been here before. But without the kind of common architecture which I've identified, the uniqueness of their vision will be invisible. In that sense, plays are like the human body. What's distinctive and unique about us is on the surface, the skin, including the most particular thing of all, the human face. Although they differ a bit, in shape and proportion, our skeletons are much less distinctive. But without our skeletons holding them up, what's unique about us would consist of indistinguishable heaps of blubber on the floor. So plays that no one else could possibly write (as no one else could look exactly like us) can nonetheless share an underlying structure. You could argue that one of the least interesting things about *King Lear* is that it shares a basic action with a fairy tale. But without that fundamental geometry in place (there's two nasty sisters and one nice one, and their father judges them wrongly), the whole thing collapses.

Like all other artists, playwrights choose, arrange, and above all concentrate events and behaviours they observe in the real world in such a way that gives them meaning. George Bernard Shaw argues that 'It is only through fiction that facts can be made instructive or even intelligible', because the writer 'rescues them from the unintelligible chaos of their actual occurrence and arranges them into works of art'.[1] How playwrights do that is the subject of this book.

Do plays have rules?

The idea of plays having shared structures is also suspect because it implies that there are rules. I touched on some of the cultural reasons for this anathema in the Preface. Many people – including many playwrights – remain attached to the romantic ideal of the uniquely expressive artist. The idea of playwriting as a craft with rules that apply over time is resisted theoretically by postmodern literary critics who believe that nothing cultural applies over time. Those playwrights who read historical criticism are understandably put off by the iron determinism of the French neoclassicist critics of the seventeenth and eighteenth centuries, with their iron laws about how many characters can be on the stage at any one time (in Vauquelin's *L'Art Poétique* it's no more than three), how long a dramatic action may be permitted to last without flouting Aristotle's unity of time (generally held to be no more than twenty-four hours), and how far distant from another a location might be without flouting Aristotle's unity of place (another room in the same house occasionally permitted, another house in the same town frowned upon, another house in another town beyond the pale).

Similarly, playwrights are alarmed by the contemporary equivalent of the French rules, those prescriptions handed out by American screenwriting experts. The founder of this school is Syd Field, who famously divided film screenplays into three acts of thirty, sixty and thirty pages, with a significant propelling plot point occurring between pages twenty-five and twenty-seven[2] (this may sound absurd, but I am assured that p. 26 of I.A.L. Diamond and Billy Wilder's script for *Some Like It Hot* includes Marilyn Monroe's character undulating unforgettably along the station platform).

More liberal – and critical of Field over such matters as the admissibility of flashbacks – is Robert McKee, whose weekend courses did so much to homogenise the vocabulary of BBC script editors in the 1980s (he has now committed the cardinal error of writing it all down[3]). But while McKee accepts what he calls open and closed endings, multiple protagonists, nonlinear time and even inconsistent realities, his definitions of 'protagonist', 'inciting incident' and 'act design' still seem schematic. And the idea that screenwriting gurus are becoming less prescriptive is countered by Blake Snyder's 2005 how-to movie-writing guide *Save the Cat!: The Last Book on Screenwriting You'll Ever Need*, with its six things that always need fixing, its nine immutable laws of movie physics, its ten genres of any movie ever made and its fifteen essential beats: from the 'Opening Image' and 'Theme Stated' via 'Fun and Games', 'Bad Guys Close In' and 'All Is Lost' to the 'Finale' and 'Final Image'.[4]

And writers who've read any twentieth-century literary theory are understandably irked by the arithmetical reductionism of so much thinking in this field, with its mechanical lists, symbols, charts and graphs.

I share some of these prejudices. But I think that the neo-classicists, Hollywood gurus and structuralist thinkers all remind us of a basic reality of playwriting, which is that, however much playwrights may choose to ignore them, audiences have certain expectations of what they're going to see in the theatre and they cannot be required to check those expectations in with their coats.

In this sense, the 'rules' are a sedimentation of all of the expectations of all the plays (and, to an extent, all the stories) which we have ever encountered. This is why the argument that one should know the rules in order to break them is only half the story. Playwrights should know the rules because they are the possession of the audience, their essential partner in the endeavour. They won't be thanked for sticking so closely to the rules that the play is predictable from start to finish. But nor will audiences readily accept their expectations being wilfully ignored.

What audiences do

The playwright Steve Gooch uses the metaphor of an arena to describe the space where plays actually happen: 'outside writer, actor and audience, and yet being the site of a common experience'.[5] The playwright David Hare sees theatre as essentially meteorological – like the weather, it happens when two fronts meet: what the actors are doing and what the audience is thinking. The literary critic J.L. Styan insists that 'the play is not on the stage but in the mind'.[6]

All I'd add to that is: not just thinking, and not only in the mind. Most writers on theatre agree that several things are happening inside us when we watch a play.

Certainly, we are empathising, identifying with and rooting for particular characters, suspending disbelief, simulating the same emotions we experience in the day-to-day: desiring, fearing, crying, shaking with laughter and shivering with fear. With the immediacy of real life (when it works), empathy invites audiences to expect: to wish or to dread. Then audiences respond – in disappointment, relief, horror or delight – to the fulfilment or denial of those expectations.

But at the same time – and it is at the same time – our brains are calling what we're watching into question. Dr Johnson's dictionary defines a play as: 'A poem in which the action is not related, but represented; and in which therefore such rules are to be observed as make the representation probable'; we apply that test to the story even as we engage with its course. As J.L. Styan puts it, 'The audience is continuously busy, whether consciously or not, making personal comparisons with what it sees and hears on the stage.'[7]

But we do more than testing what we see against personal experience. The probability that the playgoer demands is of three kinds.

The first is simple, factual **plausibility**. Does the play fit in with our knowledge of the subject or our experience of life? Do we think – or know – that policemen or hairdressers or teenagers do or don't behave like that? Are the actions of the characters reasonably justified by their circumstances? Under those circumstances, do we believe that such-and-such an outcome is feasible?

Second, we test a play for **coherence**. We ask ourselves whether it hangs together internally, whether its bits add up to a whole: whether the promise is fulfilled, the commission completed, the posed question answered. It's the impulse for coherence which explains Chekhov's rule that if you point out the gun on the wall in the first act, the audience will expect it to go off in the third.

Third, we judge a play **conventionally**, how it relates to other stage plays and indeed other fictions which we have internalised in our minds throughout our reading, listening, watching and playgoing lives. At its most basic, this is the form of probability which inclines us to expect that a tragedy will end in death and a comedy in marriage. It also leads us to suspect – and, in a way, demand – that hopes will be dashed, true love will face obstacles, rituals will be disrupted, and victory will come at a price. It's not just our expectation of internal coherence but our playgoing experience which activates the Chekhov gun rule. The audience internalises an accretion of conventions which add up to a pattern of structural expectation which can be fulfilled or broken but not ignored.

Concentration and patterns

But as our emotions empathise with the fate of the characters and our minds judge whether the matter is probable, our senses are doing something else. What we see and hear conditions our **compositional** response, allowing us to draw meaning from the patterns, shapes and rhythms which are presented to us.

In many of his theoretical writings, the director Peter Brook talks about two fundamental elements of any work of art. The first is concentration: by reducing the chaos and redundancy of the visual and aural worlds by elimination of what doesn't interest them, artists draw attention to the characteristics of what *does* interest them, including how any one element relates to the elements around it, a relationship that is often obscured in the arbitrary profusion of the real world. As Brook puts it, 'Life in the theatre is more readable and intense because it is more concentrated.'[8] Elsewhere, he explains Shakespeare's art primarily in terms of its concentration: 'Shakespeare seems better in performance than anyone else because he gives us more, moment for moment, for our money.'[9]

The second fundamental element is pattern itself. Brook is convinced that there are rules of proportion and rhythm (like the mathematical Golden Section or the rule of three) which are more fundamental than taste or culture, which touch us because they are the expression of natural laws.[10] So that, like concentration, rhythm draws attention to essences and relationships we'd otherwise miss. 'We are all aware,' he writes in *The Empty Space*, 'that most of life escapes our senses: a most powerful explanation of the various arts is that they talk of patterns which we can only begin to recognise when they manifest themselves as rhythms or shapes.'[11] Furthermore, these patterns and shapes operate between different media and are universal: 'The movement of the eye as it passes across a painting or across the vaults and arches of a great cathedral is related to a dancer's leaps and turns and to the pulse of music.'[12]

What Brook doesn't ever quite say – though I think he could – is that these two perceptions are connected. The principle by which the artist concentrates (what to eliminate, what to juxtapose) draws attention to the nature of what is being concentrated. Those principles include the hitherto invisible relationships which are exposed by concentration: the patterning of notes in music, of shapes and colours in painting, of words in scansion and rhyme.

So music is a concentration of the pitch of normal life organised by melody (change over time), rhythm (repetition over time) and harmony (things happening simultaneously). Similarly, painting organises the formless clutter of the visual world into echoing or contrasting colours and shapes. Drama borrows the patterns of other arts (the rhythm of dialogue, the balance of a stage picture) and – through the more abstract rhythms of emplotment – adds some of its own.

Drama is able to concentrate experience so effectively because of a characteristic which it shares with music, but which sets it apart from literature and painting. Because they can control the tempo of a play's consumption, dramatists can guarantee that connections are perceptible to the audience. What is intended to be a second or five minutes or an hour away from something else is going to be so. There's no marking the page, falling asleep, and picking it up again tomorrow.

This characteristic gives drama a particular power. The novelist David Lodge suggests that lyric poetry is humankind's most successful means to describe *qualia*, the raw feel of conscious awareness; while the novel is arguably the best way yet found to describe individual experience, moving through space and time.[13] Drama's capacity to point up connections is one of the reasons it has – historically – been so successful in comparing and contrasting different worlds: the objective and the subjective, the individual and the collective, the personal and the political, the worlds of the family and the state. Drama can bridge the two great sources of our experience: our direct, lived, first-person biography and the much wider range of experience and knowledge that is reported to us second- or third-hand.

In doing so, it echoes the way our memory works. We confirm the validity of a recovered memory by relating it to the real world (correspondence) but also by using it to contribute to our sense of ourselves (coherence). In that, memory echoes the external plausibility and internal coherence that we demand of drama. The fact that our sense of correspondence to reality can conflict with our desire for coherence is one of the reasons why memories are fallible.

The other analogy between memory and drama is more specific. The experience of remembering activates the same regions of the brain as the original experience. We remember the colour red by activating the same regions in the primary visual cortex as the sight of the colour activates in real life. The same neurons fire in monkeys' brains whether they're performing a task themselves or watching another monkey performing it.[14] Neurologically, the experience of seeing something enacted feels as direct – and thus as powerful – as remembering something that's happened to us. And how do we train our memory (from people's names to the order of cards in a pack)? By connecting the thing or things we want to remember with something else – say, the furniture in a room or the shape of a familiar journey – which will stimulate the same neural connection when we want to retrieve it. Like drama, memory is metonymic (we retrieve a memory from an association, recalling a romantic encounter from a whiff of perfume or the snatch of a song). But it is also connective: it exists not so much within cells, but at the synapses, the junctions between cells. In that sense, memory *is* the connection.

Patterns and culture

Much of the rest of this book will be looking at how playwrights create meaning by concentrating experience sufficiently to expose patterns and connections which audiences would otherwise miss. I need to say one other thing about those patterns. Peter Brook has been heavily criticised by multiculturalist and postmodern critics for claiming that the patterns he identifies are universal: that the shape of Notre Dame's buttresses really do share the proportions of a Japanese temple or an Arab mosque. There is an argument that we are imposing male, Western shapes (and their meanings) on discrete cultures and distinct ages: that melody and rhythm communicate different meanings in China, that the composition of a Giotto fresco didn't mean the same to fourteenth-century Tuscans as it does to us, that the meanings of particular genres are specific to the cultures which created them.

It's hard for me to judge how far culture determines the aesthetic responses of diverse communities in the world now. But I do think that – for all the manifest differences between our world and Shakespeare's – the rhythms and the patterns of his dialogue, his stage pictures and his emplotment still work as he intended them to, over four hundred years later. This could be because a recognition and appreciation of those patterns is hard-wired into us as human beings; it could equally be that they express universal human meanings (the agonies of growing up, the impermanence of love, the pain of ageing and the fear of death).

But it could also be that we recognise Shakespeare's patterns not from life but from Shakespeare, as we recognise a Beethoven phrase, which itself echoes patterns that Bach sensed in Monteverdi (and Caravaggio observed in Michelangelo and Michelangelo in Giotto). I think it's probably both: patterns develop as a way of expressing the real world, and then petrify into shapes and structures which then function independently of their original expressive purpose. Whodunnits undoubtedly express the disruption to social equilibrium caused by violent crime; but from early on the pleasure of reading them arose from the changes which writers rang on the genre. Most romantic comedies imply that the depth of a couple's love is in direct proportion to the height of the obstacles overcome to reach it; but much of the joy of reading or watching them is in the choice and structure of the barrier, and the concealment of the means by which it's going to be dismantled.

The plausibility which playgoers require connects the art to the real world; the coherence they demand makes recognisable patterns of the elements. The play's conventions relate it to other plays (and films and books and operas and paintings), which themselves created patterns and shapes in order to express something real and actual in the world.

Finally, the attention that we devote to what we see on the stage relies on the understanding that what we are seeing is mediated and intentional. If an actor plays the part with a limp, this is presumed to be telling us something about the character, not about a stumble on the stairs from the dressing room. The question 'was that part of the play?' is – essentially – distinguishing the intended (from which we are invited to draw meaning) from the accidental (which we are invited, jury-like, to exclude from our minds). Our brains are able to judge the play in this way because, however directly our emotions may be engaged, and for all our willing suspension of disbelief, in our heads we never forget it's a play. As Sir Philip Sidney reminds us:

> What child is there that, coming to a play, and seeing 'Thebes' written in great letters upon an old door, doth believe that it is Thebes?[15]

1. Quoted in Michael Holroyd, *Bernard Shaw: Volume III, The Lure of Fantasy*, London: Chatto and Windus, 1991, p. 413.

2. Syd Field, *Screenplay*, New York: Dell Trade Paperback, 1979, pp. 8-9.

3. Robert McKee, *Story*, London: Methuen, 1999.

4. Blake Snyder, *Save the Cat!: The Last Book on Screenwriting You'll Ever Need*, Studio City: Michael Wiese Productions, 2005, p. 70.

5. Steve Gooch, *Writing a Play*, London: A&C Black, 2001, p. 22.

6. J.L. Styan, *The Elements of Drama*, Cambridge: Cambridge University Press, 1960, p. 288.

7. *Ibid.* p. 235.

8. Peter Brook, *There Are No Secrets*, London: Methuen, 1993, p. 10.

9. Peter Brook, *The Shifting Point*, London: Methuen, 1987, p. 47.

10. Peter Brook, *Threads of Time*, London: Methuen, 1998, p. 133.

11. Peter Brook, *The Empty Space*, London and New York: Penguin, 1972, p. 47.

12. Peter Brook, 1998, *op. cit.*, p. 20.

13. David Lodge, *Consciousness and the Novel*, London and New York: Penguin, 2003, p. 10.

14. Steven Rose, *The 21st-Century Brain*, London: Jonathan Cape, 2009, pp. 218-9.

15. Philip Sidney, 'The Defence of Poesy', in *Sidney's 'The Defence of Poesy' and Selected Renaissance Literary Criticism*, London and New York: Penguin, 2004, p. 34.

2
Actions

Actions

Many of the terms we use to categorise the elements of dramatic fiction are slippery, and none more so than the word 'action'. Sometimes it means everything that happens on the stage ('dramatic action'), sometimes it refers narrowly to physical activity ('stage action'), or even just to the representation of violence. As a verb it's used to describe how an actor motivates an individual line. In this chapter, I'm trying to define the term, very specifically, as a brief encapsulation of the narrative progression of a play, structured to convey its meaning. In this, I am following the philosopher Aristotle.

The primacy of plot

Aristotle's *Poetics* is a problematic text. Compared to his other works, it's often elliptical in expression and sometimes inconsistent in argument. As a result of this, many scholars think it's unfinished; that it may consist of jottings or (at best) lecture notes. Only 44 pages long in the Penguin Classics edition, the book is clearly part of a larger work, which promises material on comedy (the idea that this material might have survived is the basis of the plot of Umberto Eco's medieval mystery, *The Name of the Rose*). The rules for which it's generally credited – the necessary unities of time, space and action – are taken from later interpretations, based on scant evidence in the original text (as rules, they are first formulated by Lodovico Castelvetro in an edition of 1570). Coining the expression 'Aristotalitarianism', the playwright Timberlake Wertenbaker points out that the great man's theses – such as they are – don't apply to all or even the majority of the classical Greek plays that have come down to us.

Nonetheless, Aristotle's big idea has dominated theatre criticism from his own time, via the Renaissance and the neoclassical period, through to the thinking of twentieth-century structuralist critics and on to the screenwriting gurus of our own age. That idea is that tragedy consists of 'the representation of an action', and that that action trumps everything else. His requirements of that representation are as follows:

> Tragedies are not performed, therefore, in order to represent character, though character is involved for the sake of the action... The plot, then, is the first essential of tragedy, its lifeblood, so to speak, and character takes the second place.[1]

That this is particular to drama is seen by comparing the stage to the novel. One great difference between the two media is that novelists can enter and leave their characters' heads at a twinkling; the device of free indirect speech ('What a marvellous morning it was!') allows them to dispense even with 'he thought' or 'he felt'. Thus, E.M. Forster notes, 'In the drama all human happiness and misery does and must take the form of action, otherwise its existence remains unknown, and this is the great difference between the drama and the novel.'[2] Of course, drama has developed mechanisms to cope with this limitation, including the soliloquy and the aside, and a dramatist like Chekhov uses what people say – or don't say – to imply what they are feeling with notorious ease. What drama shows us – most of the time – is what people are saying to other people, which usually means what they're doing. After all, in the original Greek, 'doing' is what drama means.

As a result (as Goethe puts it), the dramatic character acts, while the novelist's character suffers. In 1912, William Archer made the adjacent point that drama 'may be called the art of crises' while fiction was 'the art of gradual developments'.[3] Drama deals with human pain when it is made public. If, as Virginia Woolf argued, the novel is an extension of gossip, then drama is scandal writ large.

The character as function

Although not specifically concerned with drama, the early theoreticians of modernism also asserted the primacy of plot. The starting point of the thinking of the 1920s Prague School of literary criticism was the idea that fiction invites us to pay heed to hitherto familiar elements in the world by 'making them strange', through unexpected usage, framing, juxtaposition, mosaic and other defamiliarising devices. As Viktor Shklovsky put it:

> Art exists that one may recover the sensation of life; it exists to make one feel things, to make the stone *stony*.[4]

In one sense, this merely echoes Wordsworth's gentle ambition 'to give the charm of novelty to the things of everyday'. In another, it's the basis of Brecht's *Verfremdungseffekt*, usually and unhelpfully translated as 'the alienation effect' but more accurately rendered as 'estrangement', a form of stimulus which 'allows us to recognise its subject, but at the same time make it seem unfamiliar'.[5] It's a surprise to find that Brecht's starting point was not so much to make things clear, as to make them odd. But, for Brecht, recognising the oddness of things is the first step in freeing ourselves from that day-to-day numbing down of our perceptions which sees the status quo as natural and inevitable. Brecht wanted to estrange the world's doings so that we would be prodded into asking how they fitted into a pattern obscured by rhetoric, sentiment and familiarity. In that, incidentally, his purpose is distinct from that of postmodernism, which claims that there isn't a pattern at all.

The second ambition of the Russian formalists and the Prague School was to find the underlying patterns in narrative fiction. Their crucial distinction (one that now seems utterly commonplace) is between what they called the **story** (or *fabula*), the bare, chronological succession of events drawn on in a fiction; and **plot** (or *sjuzet*), the events as they are ordered and connected. Like rhyme and scansion in poetry, this ordering estranges the raw material, and draws attention to its underlying meaning. From that perception, they and their successors sought to analyse how stories work.

The first systematic attempt to categorise the elements of story was undertaken by the French theorist Georges Polti, who in 1921 published *The Thirty-Six Dramatic Situations*, whose number is echoed – in 'a singular corollary' – by 'the discovery that there are in life but thirty-six emotions'.[6] The flavour of the situations can be detected from numbers one to ten: Supplication, Deliverance, Crime Pursued by Vengeance, Vengeance Taken for Kindred upon Kindred, Pursuit, Disaster, Falling Prey to Cruelty or Misfortune, Revolt, Daring Enterprise and Abduction. Each situation contains a number of alternative scenarios (in Crime Pursued by Vengeance, they include the Avenging of a Slain Parent or Ancestor, Vengeance for Having Been Despoiled During Absence and Revenge Upon a Whole Sex for a Deception by One, of which Polti gives the example of Jack the Ripper). Each situation also requires a number of elements, some of which are abstract forces (like Punishment, Remembrance of the Victim, or a Vanquished Power), but most of which are embodied as characters defined by their place in the action (from an Unfortunate, a Threatener and a Rescuer in Deliverance to a Tyrant and a Conspirator in Revolt).

The idea that characters are an embodiment of forces that are present in a number of stories is explored in more detail by Vladimir Propp, whose 1928 *Morphology of the Folktale* sought to analyse the plots of just over a hundred Russian folktales, taken reasonably arbitrarily from a book of five hundred such tales (Propp studied numbers fifty to one hundred and fifty-one inclusive). From this study, Propp concluded that, while 'the names of the dramatis personae change (as well as the attributes of each)', neither their actions nor their functions change. 'From this,' he concluded, 'we can draw the inference that a tale often attributes identical actions to various personages. This makes possible the study of the tale *according to the functions of its dramatis personae*.'[7]

By analysing the stories not through the relations of individual characters but through the interaction of character functions, Propp realised that, in essence, all folk stories embrace or select from one story, which goes like this:

A merchant, father or king dies or departs, leaving behind him an injunction (don't look in the cupboard, don't go into the forest, don't open the box, read the book, or eat the apple).

This injunction is violated, which leads to the appearance of a villain, who steals or harms a person or their belongings. A hero is commissioned to defeat the villain and to rescue his victim. Journeying to meet the villain, the hero comes across a personage who engages (or entraps) him into a task, for which he receives a reward whose value is not immediately apparent but which becomes crucial later on (it may be a steed to get to the villain, or a weapon, or a magic object, or a skill like being able to speak to animals). Arriving at the villain, the hero employs his magic weapon to defeat him. He returns home, only to find he has been usurped in his absence and his identity is denied. The hero then proves his identity by the passing of a seemingly impossible test of strength or endurance (in *The Odyssey* by pulling a great bow; in the Christian story by rising from the dead), he wins his bride and comes into his kingdom.

Propp's point is that 'the number of functions is extremely small, whereas the number of personages is extremely large'.[8] For example, the personage from whom the hero wins his vital weapon could be an old woman, a witch, a group of knights, a robber, an animal or even a river or a tree. In the Hindu epic *The Ramayana* it's a wise man who gives Rama a magic arrow; in the Brothers Grimms' tale of three brothers it's the dogs who teach the youngest brother how to bark; in the James Bond movies it's Q, the gadget demonstrator. In C.S. Lewis's *The Lion, the Witch and the Wardrobe*, the magic weapons with which Peter, Susan, Edmund and Lucy will defeat the White Witch are distributed by Father Christmas from his sleigh. Sometimes the donor can be unaware of his donation. Often the detective's dim-witted but good-hearted sidekick accidentally provides the clue which unlocks the mystery. In a TV advertisement, an engineer works out how to service several oil wells from one platform when he sees his son drink a milkshake through a bendy straw.

Propp argues that the 'definition of a function will most often be given in the form of a noun expressing an action';[9] if not a single word like Interdiction or Violation, then a description (a task is commissioned, a task is performed; a contract/promise is made, kept or broken). From his analysis of the stories, he identified thirty-one character functions, which he grouped into seven spheres of action, and from which storytellers have fashioned a virtual infinity of characters: the villain, the hero, the helper, the donor, the sought-for person (the victim) and their father, the despatcher of the hero, and the false hero.

Subsequently, a number of critics sought to revise and develop Propp's ideas. In 1950, the French drama theorist Etienne Souriau defined six plot functions with charming astrological names (Lion=hero, Sun=value to be sought, Earth=receiver, Mars=opponent, Scale=arbiter, Moon=helper), and from them deduced precisely 210,141 dramatic situations, or horoscopes, by combining these codes algebraically. Later on, A.J. Greimas returned to folktales in his 1966 *Structural Semantics*, defining six plot functions called actants (sender/receiver, subject/object, helper/opponent). As in Propp's spheres of action, Greimas' actants are not descriptions of individual, discrete characters. Some actants may be a group (Cleopatra has lots of helpers, and a hero can be a team, as in *The Great Escape* or *Seven Samurai*). A character may fulfil more than one function (a protagonist may send him or herself in pursuit of an object). A character might well shift category, as Buckingham, Enobarbus and Mosca shift from being Richard III, Antony and Volpone's helpers to being their opponents. The absence of a particular actant in a story might well be crucial to its outcome: neither Hedda Gabler nor Nora Helmer (in Ibsen's *A Doll's House*) have any helpers at all.

Through his study of character functions, Greimas found three basic plot forms in folktales:

- The **contractual**, in which the hero enters into a contract, keeps it or breaks it (from *The Merchant of Venice* via *Faust* to *The Pied Piper of Hamelin*).

- The **performative**, in which the hero agrees or decides to perform a task or submit to a trial (from *The Book of Job* via *Hamlet* to *The Good Person of Setzuan*).

- And, third, what Greimas calls the **disjunctive** structure, which is based round movement, journeying, departure and arrival: the quest story (from *The Odyssey* and *The Aeneid* via *Henry V* and *Pericles* to *The Caucasian Chalk Circle*).

It is obviously true that these categories are not mutually exclusive. Heroes can be contracted to perform a task which involves a journey, and they often are.

A less abstract and more empirical way of analysing plot is by summary. The playwright Stephen Jeffreys lists the proverbial seven basic plots as that of *Cinderella* (virtue finally recognised), Achilles (the hero with a fatal flaw), *Faust* (the debt that must be paid), *Tristan and Isolde* (the eternal triangle), Circe (the spider and the fly), Orpheus (the gift withdrawn), and *Romeo and Juliet* (boy meets girl). The writer Christopher Booker has come up with an overlapping list in his *The Seven Basic Plots*: Overcoming the Monster, Rags to Riches, The Quest, Voyage and Return, Comedy, Tragedy and Rebirth.[10]

The difference between the character function and the seven-plot model is that the latter defines the narrative in terms of its meaning. In that, it approaches what I'm defining as an action. Aristotle himself defines 'action' as a progression, its necessary wholeness consisting in its having a beginning, a middle and an end. For me, an action is the formula which transforms *fabula* into *szujet*, providing the principles by which the story is structured into a plot. Or, put the other way round, the plot is the way the story is presented dramatically in order to reveal an action.

Actions in theory

So what does an action give the story? First of all, it provides causality. As E.M. Forster puts it: 'The king died and the queen died' is story; 'The king died and then the queen died of grief' is plot. But in many post-Aristotelian attempts to define an action, there is another element: the idea that the dramatic action expresses not just a progression of cause and effect, but a contradiction in the human condition. For the eighteenth-century German critic Wilhelm Schlegel, the tragic subject is our baffled response to the contrast between our longing for the infinite and our finite limitations.[11] In that, he anticipates twentieth-century critics like James Feibleman, who sees drama as being about the disjuncture between the actual and possible, and Martha C. Nussbaum, who sees tragedy as 'a struggle between the ambition to transcend the merely human and a recognition of the losses entailed by this ambition'.[12] For David Mamet, drama poses questions whose 'complexity and depth' renders them 'unsusceptible to rational examination'.[13]

For these critics, an action is not about completion but an acknowledgement of various kinds of failure. The gap between our knowledge of the infinite and our finite lives is an irony, and it is this irony which is at the core of a minor but – in seeking to define actions – instructive art form: the tag lines on movie posters. Tag lines seek to express the essential appeal of a movie in a phrase which pithily encapsulates its theme, its interest and its mood. This form embraces a number of techniques:

- **The Rule of Three**, including: 'Trapped in time. Surrounded by evil. Low on gas' (*Army of Darkness*); 'Small town, big crime, dead cold' (*Fargo*); 'Movies were his passion. Women were his inspiration. Angora sweaters were his weakness' (*Ed Wood*); 'For better. For worse. Forever' (*Tom and Viv*).

- **Wordplay**, as in: 'His Majesty was all-powerful and all-knowing. But he wasn't quite all there' (*The Madness of King George*); 'Paul Sheldon used to write for a living. Now he's writing to stay alive' (*Misery*); 'They overcame the impossible by doing the unthinkable' (*Alive*).

- **Contradictions**, such as: 'They're having a secret love affair. Only 50,000 people know about it' (*Aunt Julia and the Scriptwriter*); 'Fifty million people watched. But no one saw a thing' (*Quiz Show*).

- **Twists**, like: 'In the Wild West a woman had only two choices. She could be a wife or she could be a whore... Josephine Monaghan chose to be a man' (*The Ballad of Little Jo*).

What all of these tag lines and hundreds of others demonstrate is that the hook is in the twist. In almost all the above cases, the last beat of the sentence changes our take on the material, indicating how a banal, commonplace situation (a secret love affair, someone writing for a living) will be enriched, complicated or challenged by an incongruity or a contradiction. That this model can express contradictions as profound as those cited by Wilhelm Schlegel is shown by these examples:

1) The first person you want to trust, the last person you want to suspect (*The Hawk*).

2) Everything that makes him dangerous makes her love him even more (*Mr Jones*).

3) Evil is irresistible (*Mary Reilly*).

4) When the law can't protect the innocent... it takes an outlaw to deliver justice (*Nowhere to Run*).

5) Sooner or later a man who wears two faces forgets which one is real (*Primal Fear*).

6) When you go undercover, remember one thing: who you are (*ID*).

The first encapsulates the paradox of the kind or seemingly kind villain (from Iago to the old ladies in *Arsenic and Old Lace*), the second and third the sexual attraction of delinquency (from Edmund in *King Lear* to Heathcliff in *Wuthering Heights*). The fourth sums up the irony of revenge drama and the hard-boiled thriller. The last two express the danger that, from Prince Hal and Hamlet onwards, the impostor will forget that he is imposturing, and become his disguise. All of them address, in different ways, the gap between the ideal and the real, expressed in a twist. In that, they're a model for the formulation of a dramatic action.

A dramatic action consists of a **project** (usually described in the form of a subject, verb and object: someone sets out to do something), followed by a **contradiction** or **reversal** (as like as not a clause beginning with the word 'but'). So, the project of the Achilles story is his mother's ambition to arm him for a life of military glory; but her means of doing this is the very thing which brings about his untimely death. Marlowe's Doctor Faustus (though not Goethe's) seeks everything he wants in this world, but at the price of eternal sacrifice in the next one. In order to achieve its objective, the fly sacrifices its independence to the spider; Orpheus makes a huge effort to rescue Eurydice, but his work is wasted by one last, tiny mistake. In both the tragic romance and the eternal triangle, love aspires to conquer all, but ends up conquered, from without or from within.

This is a model of actions of plays with tragic or ironic endings, from 'A general comes back in triumph from the war, but is killed by his vengeful wife' all the way to 'Two men wait for a third man, but he doesn't arrive'. There is an alternative model of the action, which applies fully to only one of the usually cited seven plots (though to more of Christopher Booker's). Despite the efforts of her jealous elder sisters, Cinderella nonetheless goes to the ball and wins the prince. Similarly, the basic action of new comedy is that, 'despite the objections of her parents, a young woman nonetheless wins the man she loves'. However, a shadow of the 'project but reversal' action often lurks behind the cheerful 'despite... nonetheless' model. Cinderella wins her prince, but at the price of her sisters' humiliation. In achieving their romantic ambitions, the young couple may have sacrificed more than they know.

Axis and currency

In identifying the action of complicated narratives, notably those without a clear individual protagonist, it's helpful to identify two other elements. The first is the play's **axis**, the line of conflict between the opposing principles in the play. Examples include:

– The conflict between justice and mercy, implying that revenge can be worse than the original crime – the axis of the Renaissance revenge drama, and countless thrillers, Westerns and spy movies in our own time.

– The trade-off between truth and harm, implying that the exposure of truth can cause more damage than its concealment – the axis of Ibsen's *The Wild Duck*, J.B. Priestley's *Dangerous Corner*, J.M. Synge's *The Well of the Saints*, Terence Rattigan's *In Praise of Love* and Yasmina Reza's *Art*.

- The contradiction between desire and duty (the axis at the heart of most traditional love stories) and the link between oppression and dependence (you can't live with someone, but you can't live without them) which is at the core of many modern ones.

- The disparity between expectations and results – acting to bring about one end, only to bring about another; or achieving what you aimed for, but finding it isn't what you wanted after all. One version of this, the Midas plot – the curse of getting what you want – lies at the heart of most of the great tales of villainy.

- And, in our own age, the clash of character and circumstance – the axis along which, in their different ways, the characters of Ibsen, Chekhov, Shaw, Brecht and Beckett negotiate modernity.

Complementing the concept of the axis is the notion of **currency** – what the play (and on occasions an entire opus) deals in. The nineteenth-century realists are particularly clear: most Ibsen plays deal in the currency of exposure (of the past); most Chekhov plays are about coping with the loss of a wished-for future. Shaw's great subject was disenchantment, though, as he pointed out, you can't be disenchanted unless you're enchanted first.

Actions as interpretation

Some people argue that actions are specific to the times in which they are coined; that they are an act of interpretation rather than analysis. In a secular age, *Macbeth* appears to be the story of a soldier sacrificing his moral scruples to achieve his objective, but finding that his ambitions will always outreach him; but you could also see it as a Christian allegory. *Hamlet* can be read as a Freudian story, in which 'a son seeks to avenge one parent, but fails because of his feelings for his other parent'. Nahum Tate's eighteenth-century subtitle for *Coriolanus* – 'The Ingratitude of a Commonwealth' – implies a very different meaning for the play from the one we've grown accustomed to.

In a 1592 commentary on *Romeo and Juliet*, Arthur Brooke argued that the play presented the cautionary tale of 'a couple of unfortunate lovers, thralling themselves to unhonest desire; neglecting the authority and advice of parents and friends; conferring their principal counsels with drunken gossips and superstitious friars, etc.'.[14] When it was written in the early 1980s, Caryl Churchill's *Top Girls* seemed to be about the perceived conflict between the aims of feminism and the ideals of socialism, and you could action it as: 'To succeed as an individual, a woman denies that she is oppressed as a class.' A decade later, David Mamet's *Oleanna* – a play about a female student accusing a lecturer of sexual harrassment – was read in radically different ways by those who backed the student and those who sided with the lecturer.

The most powerful evidence for the relativist case is provided by Sophocles' *Antigone*. Hegel saw drama in general and *Antigone* in particular as being about the irreconcilable tragic conflict between the absolute right of the family and the absolute right of the state. For other critics in other times the play has been seen as confronting the axes of community versus blood, culture versus nature, law versus passion, expediency versus integrity, and, in the 1960s, rebellion versus oppression.

But however disputed and disputable these various readings may be, the play's meaning is demonstrated by the way it's put together. As we shall see later, the actions of *Top Girls* and *Oleanna* are revealed by their structure; as the actions of both *Antigone* and *Oedipus* are revealed by Sophocles' means of emplotment.

Emplotment: time

There are two chief ways in which emplotment expresses the action of a play: plotting by time (by ordering the events of the story), and, second, plotting by space (juxtaposing its different strands).

Almost all plays start some way into the story, and thus involve exposition, the revelation of what's happened before. The choice between starting late or starting early may be informed by the political and cultural context in which plays are performed, the preferred length of plays in a particular era, the shape of theatre buildings, the mechanisms of theatrical production, the hold of tradition or the pull of the new. However, whether constrained by the custom of the times or enabled by the free decision of the playwright, the choice of how the story is expressed in the plot goes way beyond storytelling convenience. Emplotment gives meaning.

One of the best examples is one of the earliest. Chronologically, the story of Sophocles' *Oedipus* goes like this:

1) King Laius and Queen Jocasta of Thebes have a son.

2) Apollo's oracle warns that the son is destined to kill his father and marry his mother.

3) To avoid this fate, Laius and Jocasta instruct a servant to take the child, to pierce its feet with an iron pin, and to abandon it on a mountainside to die.

4) The child is rescued and taken to Corinth, where he is adopted by King Polybus and his queen.

5) Called Oedipus ('swollen foot'), the boy grows up and learns of the prediction concerning his future. To avoid his fate, he flees from the king and queen whom he believes to be his parents. His journeyings bring him to Thebes.

6) On the outskirts of the city, he has an altercation with an old man and kills him.

7) He discovers Thebes in panic and peril; its king has been killed and the city is in the grip of the monstrous Sphinx.

8) Oedipus outwits the Sphinx, is made King of Thebes and marries Jocasta, its queen.

9) After fifteen years of prosperity, plague and famine have returned to Thebes.

10) Oedipus is told that the city will never recover unless the identity of the killer of its former king is discovered. He determines to identify the murderer, even when he learns

that his investigation will reveal shocking news about his own identity.

11) Oedipus finds out that the old man he killed on the outskirts was Laius, that he was Laius's son, and that his wife Jocasta is his mother.

12) Jocasta kills herself. Oedipus puts out his own eyes, and leaves to wander the earth with his daughters.

As Sophocles has written the play, the plot is the last four elements, revealing the first eight. The action is: 'To save his city, the king seeks the identity of the author of a crime, but he discovers in the end that it is himself.'

But had Sophocles emplotted the story chronologically, the action would be different. The protagonists of the chronological plot would be the parents, and the action would be something like: 'Threatened with the prediction that their son will commit two terrible crimes, a king and queen decide to take extreme measures; but the fates are too strong for them, and the prediction is fulfilled despite their efforts.' Laius and Jocasta's story is about how you can't avoid fate, however much you try. Whereas by starting with Oedipus, the play becomes about human volition; the message changes from 'you can't win', to 'leave well alone'.

Oedipus demonstrates, in one of its purest forms, the effect of starting late. This strategy works – it only works, in fact – when it involves 'the past coming to life in the present and creating drama' (as Arthur Miller's playwriting tutor Kenneth Rowe taught him). For director Michael Blakemore, the technique works because, by working on the present, the past determines the future (Oedipus's doom).[15] The backstory is not something we need to know before the present-tense story can begin; its revelation *is* the drama because it brings about what happens in front of us and what will happen after the curtain falls.

As Blakemore points out, this is Ibsen's basic technique. After *Peer Gynt*, most of Ibsen's plays cover no more than a couple of days; *John Gabriel Borkman* is pretty much in real time. But an Ibsen *story* starts years and years before. Almost every mature Ibsen plot hinges on a revelation from the past; the actions of *Pillars of the Community*, *A Doll's House*, *Ghosts*,

The Lady from the Sea, Hedda Gabler, The Master Builder and *Borkman* are all provoked by people returning from the past and bringing revelations with them.

By contrast, the plays of Shakespeare rarely involve revelations from the past, and have little backstory. In truth, Shakespeare wasn't skilled at exposition, and didn't get much better at it as his career went on, which is a comfort to the rest of us. Both *The Comedy of Errors* (written at the beginning of his career) and *The Tempest* (written at the end) have huge expository speeches explaining what the audience needs to know to follow the rest of the play. In *The Comedy of Errors*, the scene is a 'dialogue' between two minor characters, in which Egeon explains the separated-twin pairing at the core of the plot, helped along by the Duke of Ephesus's occasional prompting. In the second scene of *The Tempest*, Prospero explains the circumstances of his deposition and banishment to his daughter Miranda. Great actors can make these speeches memorable in other ways, but it's hard to be interested in characters whom we have yet to meet (in *The Comedy of Errors*) or whom we've only seen shouting in the eye of a storm. Usually, Shakespeare's present tense is just that: the crucial decisions of all the characters take place before our very eyes.

For Bertolt Brecht, this form of playwriting was both a method and a theory. Brecht wrote in the present tense because he wanted us to ask, moment by moment, whether his characters could have behaved differently. It's more than an enjoyable parlour game to imagine how Brecht would write an Ibsen play, and vice versa. In Brecht's *The Life of Galileo*, we see the great scientist take a series of crucial decisions, from his claim to have invented the telescope to his renunciation of his writings before the Inquisition. In the penultimate scene, many years after his recantation, one of Galileo's former pupils comes to see him under what is effectively house arrest near Florence. At first, we are invited to believe that Galileo's recantation was a wily dance-step, allowing him to survive his persecution and carry on his revolutionary scientific work (indeed, this is the conclusion of Brecht's first draft of the play). But then Galileo turns the tables, declaring that he could and should have acted differently. His denial of the truth made him intolerable in the ranks of science.

The plot of Ibsen's *Ghosts* also turns on the denial of a truth. Ten years after the death of his father, Oswald has come home to see his mother, Mrs Alving, who is setting up an orphanage with the puritanical Pastor Manders in memory of her husband. We learn that, far from being the upstanding paragon Oswald believes him to be, Captain Alving was a promiscuous drunkard (he fathered the household's current maid) and Mrs Alving once wanted to leave him for the Pastor, but was refused. Now Mrs Alving has to decide whether to tell Oswald the truth about his father. Before this can happen, Oswald tells his mother that he's contracted syphilis, of which he is mortally ashamed, not least for having let down his father's memory. After news arrives that the orphanage is on fire (through Manders' carelessness with candle shavings), Mrs Alving tells Oswald the truth: he contracted syphilis from his father; she will look after him as he dies.

In the Brecht version of *Ghosts*, the two big decisions (Oswald's to admit to his syphilis, and Mrs Alving's to tell the truth about his father) would be but the last of a whole series. We would start – at the very latest – with Mrs Alving's proposal to Pastor Manders and his refusal. We would probably travel with Oswald to Paris, and certainly we would see Mrs Alving deciding to continue to lavish praise on her reprobate husband in her letters. Maybe we'd witness Oswald's minor debauchery and the embarrassing interview with the doctor somewhere discreet on the Left Bank. The play as we have it would be the last couple of scenes. Oswald and Mrs Alving's decisions to come clean would be balanced by our knowledge of her and Pastor Manders' previous decisions to lie.

By contrast, Ibsen's *Galileo* would all be in the second-to-last scene. We would see none of Galileo's earlier actions, and so wouldn't consider how they might have been different. Having missed Galileo's earlier, wily footwork, we'd be less interested in the possibility that his recantation was all a device. We would be primarily interested in his former pupil's need to believe that it was a device, and in Galileo's determination to be honest about his betrayal. The play wouldn't be about a decision in the past to deny the truth, a decision that could have gone the other way, but a decision to admit the truth about that decision. In the present tense of the play, what we'd see is two men coming to terms.

Far from using different mechanisms to the same end, Brecht's *Ghosts* and Ibsen's *Galileo* would be different plays, with different meanings.

Emplotment: space

If time emplotment reveals meaning by putting events in a particular order, then space emplotment works by juxtaposition.

The most obvious example in Shakespeare is the use of the subplot. Shakespeare clearly invites us to look for a common dramatic action in his main and his subplots, and to draw the inference that that action is his principal concern. The fact that *Hamlet* is about the means by which a man avenges the death of his father (and not about, say, a man in love with his mother or the daughter of his father's councillor) is demonstrated not by a careful reading of other Elizabethan verse dramas, nor by an understanding of how Shakespeare has been read in particular periods since. It's shown by there being three men who set out to avenge their father's deaths (Hamlet himself, Laertes and Fortinbras), and, hence, by almost all the stage action consisting of one or other of them pursuing that objective, in radically contrasting ways.

Similarly, the idea that *King Lear* is about a man misjudging what his children tell him is demonstrated by the fact that the same thing happens both in the main and in the subplot: Gloucester believes that his scheming bastard son Edmund is telling the truth, and that his younger son Edgar is lying. That we are invited to compare the two men's understanding as well as their misunderstanding is shown in Act 4, in which Gloucester serves as the mad Lear's wits, and Lear as the blind Gloucester's eyes. At the beginning of the play, two good if flawed old men get it wrong, and three bad young people get it right. At the end of the play the situation is reversed.

Shakespeare mirrors his plots and subplots again and again. In *Much Ado About Nothing*, Hero and Claudio are broken apart by malicious lies while Beatrice and Benedick are brought together by benign deceit. The two plots of *The*

Merchant of Venice both involve good people swearing oaths to uphold bad laws.

Similarly, in Wilde's *The Importance of Being Earnest*, we find the action of the play when we ask what its two male protagonists have in common: we find that both Jack and Algernon create a world of fantasy in order to evade the social limitations of their daily lives, but both find that their imaginary worlds can be made real through love. The action of *Three Sisters* could centre on Andrei's gauche and gawky young wife Natasha ('A woman marries above herself into a family which patronises her; but gradually she takes over the family home and is the only person to achieve her goals'). The fact that it isn't is demonstrated by more than the title. We know the play is about failed rather than achieved ambitions because that condition applies – in its different ways – to all three sisters and their brother.

There are countless examples of the use of juxtaposition to reveal meaning in contemporary plays. Peter Shaffer's *Equus*, Bryony Lavery's *Frozen* and Joe Penhall's *Blue/Orange* are all about psychiatrists who deny problems they share with the people they're counselling. Another striking example of how mirrored plots convey meaning is Roy Williams' *Little Sweet Thing*, a play in which a young black criminal tries to go straight but fails. The variant here is that the young man whose action pulls the protagonist back into crime is one of two white characters who hero-worship and then emulate black role models. The subplot variant of this main action involves a weak white girl who's bullied by a lippy black girl, eventually taking on the black girl's clothes, style and language and thereby turning the tables on her. Structurally, the common action of the two plots (weak white people emulate strong black people, making them harder but nastier) points to Williams's meaning.

Sometimes, time emplotment works hand-in-hand with space emplotment to display the action. In *Oedipus*, there are two pairs of mirrored actions, speaking to each of the two possible emplotments of the story. In order to evade his fate, Oedipus leaves two cities; once when his real parents commission their servant to abandon him to his death; second, when he learns of the oracle's prediction himself, and leaves his adoptive parents in Corinth. There are also two characters who seek to take command of their fate, thereby bringing about the end they want most to avoid: the Corinthian shepherd who decides to rescue Oedipus sets the tragic chain of events in motion; Oedipus's decision to find out Laius's murderer's identity brings the play to its terrible climax.

Finally, returning to *Antigone*, we find that here, too, the mirroring of two plots unlocks the action of the play. However its axis might have been read by different audiences at different times, the action is consistent. Creon privileges the needs of the state over the obligations of kinship twice, once by intention, the second time by effect. His determination to condemn Antigone to death for burying her brother Polynices leads to the suicide of his own son. The action of the play is this: 'A king condemns his predecessor's rebellious daughter to death in order to preserve civil concord; but, in doing so, he brings about the death of his own son.'

The two basic actions

There is one final proposition about actions. Michael Eaton argues that all plots are variants of odd couples and fish out of water; Stephen Lowe thinks all plays are about people escaping or invading secure communities. I think that actions ultimately boil down to two: again, one to do with time and one with space. Both dimensions imply an action which fulfils David Mamet's definition of great drama, in that they confront those contradictions in the human condition that are not ultimately subject to a rational solution.

First, the **Time Action**. Operating vertically, onwards through time, the project of this action is the achievement of our limitless ambitions, but the reversal is that these ambitions are inevitably going to be thwarted by our finite nature. The first story in the Bible – Adam and Eve – is an emplotment of the time action. In all of its many manifestations, the message of the Fall trumps the message of the Resurrection.

The **Space Action** is also about failure, but operating horizontally, across the gap between ourselves and others. We think we know our neighbour as ourself but we don't. We try to be at one with the other but we never can. The fascination of playwrights throughout the ages with reunited twins is a result of the power of this action. Our failure to love our brother as ourself is, of course, the thrust of the second human story in the Bible, that of Cain and Abel. As Eric Bentley puts it: 'Our identification of ourselves with others' makes of our lives 'one long attempt to reverse the universal failure'.[16] But sometimes comedy hints that, while we'll never be at one, we can get closer to each other than we think.

There will be more on emplotment as a tool for expressing meaning, seen through the prism of genre and the practicalities of structure. But, before that, I want to look at an element of plays which has taken a back seat in this chapter.

1. Aristotle, 'Poetics' in *Classical Literary Criticism*, trans. T.S. Dorsch, London and New York: Penguin, 1965, p. 40.

2. E.M. Forster, *Aspects of the Novel*, New York: Harvest, 1985, p. 84.

3. Quoted in Marvin Carlson, *Theories of the Theatre*, Ithaca, New York: Cornell University Press, 1984, p. 309.

4. Quoted in Elaine Aston and George Savona, *Theatre as Sign-System*, London: Routledge, 1991, p. 7.

5. *Ibid.*

6. Georges Polti, *The Thirty-Six Dramatic Situations*, trans. Lucille Ray, Boston: Writer Inc., 1977, p. 9.

7. Vladimir Propp, *Morphology of the Folktale*, trans. Laurence Scott, revised Louis A.Wagner, Austin, Texas: University of Texas Press, 1968, p. 20.

8. *Ibid.*

9. *Ibid.* p. 21.

10. Christopher Booker, *The Seven Basic Plots*, New York: Continuum, 2004.

11. Marvin Carlson, *op. cit.*, p. 178.

12. Martha C. Nussbaum, *The Fragility of Goodness: Luck and Ethics in Greek Tragedy and Philosophy*, Cambridge: Cambridge University Press, 1986, p. 8.

13. David Mamet, *Writing in Restaurants*, London and New York: Penguin, 1986, p. 8.

14. Quoted in Carlson, *op. cit.*, p. 78.

15. Martin Gottfried, *Arthur Miller: A Life*, London: Faber and Faber, 2003, p. 35.

16. Eric Bentley, *The Life of the Drama*, London: Methuen, 1965, p. 178.

3
Character

3

Character

Character

I've argued that Aristotle is right in his claim that plot is 'the first essential of tragedy', and character takes the second place. There is, of course, a contrary view, starting from the premise that the mainspring of drama is not plot but character. Historically, the debate over character in drama is the debate between classicism and modernism on the one hand, and romanticism and realism on the other.

For the Roman critics who built on Aristotle, the genre of a play depended not just on the outcome of the plot but on the social rank of its characters. So, tragedy involved high-placed persons to whom the audience looks up, and comedy middle and low life, on whom the audience looks down. Hence, the prologue of Plautus's *Amphitryon* defines the play as tragicomedy because it includes characters drawn from across the social spectrum: gods, kings and servants. Further, Roman critics developed a concept of 'decorum', tangentially connected to decorum in the sense we understand it, connecting characters' rank and office with their behaviour. So Plutarch criticises Aristophanes for giving out lines 'as if by lot' to sons, fathers, peasants, gods, old men and heroes. The poet should by the rules of decorum seek a proper quality for each: 'State to a prince, force to an orator, innocence to a woman, meanness of language to a poor man, and sauciness to a tradesman.'[1]

This stricture was taken up by neoclassical critics in Italy and France. In 1555, Jacques Peletier insisted that in comedy, old men must be avaricious or prudent, young men ardent and loving, nurses diligent, mothers indulgent. This notion was not confined to the continent. In 1578, George Whetstone condemned English drama not only for its rejection of the

Aristotelian unities of place, time and action but in giving 'one order of speach for all persons'.[2] In this, these critics echoed Aristotle's view that it was not 'appropriate that a female character should be given manliness or cleverness'.[3]

The classical and romantic character

These theories are echoed, of course, in practical observation of genres. Although some have professions and others ranks, the figures in Italian *Commedia dell'Arte* are essentially defined by their theatrical role, as in the deceived father Pantalone, the various lovers (*Innamorati*), the overlooked Pedrolino, the thieving Scaramuccia, the stammering Tartaglia, and, within the servant classes, the manipulative Brighella, the unrequited Arlecchino, the scampering Scapino and the sensible Colombina. Some of the *Commedia* figures translate into other cultures: Pedrolino becomes the French Pierrot and Pulcinella our Mr Punch. Many of their routines can be detected in other dramatic genres: the confusion between two soldiers that leads to Sir Andrew Aguecheek's beating by Sebastian in *Twelfth Night* is a version of a routine involving the braggart Capitano and the genuinely courageous Cavaliero; Tartaglia's stammering shows up in the malapropisms of Dogberry in *Much Ado About Nothing* and Elbow in *Measure for Measure*.[4]

Similarly, the figures in broadcast soap opera are defined partially by profession, office, rank and relation, but also (and often principally) by role. Hence the observation that the loss of a particular character (through story development or an actor leaving the series) may require the introduction of a different character to perform the same character function, whether that of the crusty if benign old Patriarch, the Busybody, the Leader-astray, the False Friend, the Pillar of the Community, the Stud, the Vixen, the Tragedy Queen, the Joker or the Shoulder-to-cry-on. Indeed, in seeking to define the *roles* in soap opera, one finds oneself producing categories that echo Polti's dramatic elements (threateners, rescuers, conspirators). Sometimes such stereotypes can be employed so often that they become archetypes, roles which operate across cultures. Certainly, the writers of screenwriting manuals are happy to identify certain types of person as archetypes; in *The Complete Writer's Guide to Heroes and Heroines*, Tami D. Cowden, Caro LaFever and Sue Viders identify what they see as a complete list of male archetypes, consisting of the Chief, Bad Boy, Best Friend, Charmer, Lost Soul, Professor, Swashbuckler and Warrior; complemented by the female Boss, Seductress, Spunky Kid, Free Spirit, Waif, Librarian, Crusader and Nurturer, going on to describe the dramatic potential of seventy-two paired and twelve ensemble interactions between them.[5] In this, of course, they too echo those twentieth-century structuralists – from Vladimir Propp between the wars to Souriau and Greimas after it – who see individual characters as the expression of a much smaller number of character functions or – in Greimas's formulation – actants.

Between the neoclassicists and the modern world, however, sit the romantics and realists, whose work defines most of the theatre of the twentieth century, and for whom character could not be seen in these terms. The *Commedia* actors called their roles 'masks', and it's possible to see the story of drama from *Commedia* to Chekhov as the supplanting of the mask by the face. The literary critic John Lennard argues that Shakespeare's characters were based on a conflation of medieval vices and the stock figures of Roman comedy, which gradually broke free of their origins; so that while Falstaff is a recognisable *miles gloriosus* (boastful soldier) and Shylock a *senex* (old man) or Pantaloon, King Lear is an old man who commands our empathy as well as our pity. By the late nineteenth century, Ibsen is describing his characters not as actors in a drama but as persons of his aquaintance: in the first draft, they are strangers on a train; in the second, people one had known for a few weeks at a spa; by the last draft, 'they are my intimate friends, they will not disappoint me, I shall always see them as I now do'.[6] What Ibsen is describing, of course, is the individuality, specificity and uniqueness of his creations. The early twentieth-century British realist John Galsworthy insisted that 'a human being is the best plot there is... The dramatist who hangs his characters to his plot, instead of hanging his plot to his characters, is guilty of cardinal sin.'[7] Similarly, Harold Pinter explained how he had originally conceived of his play *The Caretaker* ending with the violent death of one of the three characters at the hands of another. But, when he got to the point, the characters that he had created just wouldn't act that way.

However, in creating fully fledged and rounded characters, playwrights are severely restricted. Unlike novelists, they can present their characters to the public only through what they say and do. And however individual their behaviour, characters are not in fact free-standing; however much they strut and fret, they do so for an hour, upon a stage. Ibsen may get to know his characters better than his family, but the audience enjoys their society not for a few weeks at a spa, but for three hours in a darkened playhouse. Indeed, not even three: put together, the entire part of Hamlet could be quoted at reasonable speed between Coventry and London on the train.

Further, we make these people's fleeting acquaintance within the particular conditions of the drama. More strictly than the plays which contain them, characters have beginnings, middles and ends. We learn about characters by way of introduction, then through their pursuit of an objective, and finally by their success or failure in achieving it. The invention and development of characters – including the means to make them arresting, engaging and memorable – are all constrained within those narrow confines, whether we like it or not.

Building characters

Introductions

Apart from Richard II and Richard III (who open their plays), there is no Shakespearian tragic hero who is not introduced before his first entrance. Hamlet is discussed by the soldiers on the battlements, Othello by Iago and Roderigo, and Macbeth by the witches and Duncan. Before Lear's arrival, Kent and Gloucester have speculated as to his intentions, and before Timon enters, we have learnt of his generosity and suspect he's being taken for a ride. When we meet him, Caius Martius has already been dubbed the chief enemy of the people (though not yet dubbed Coriolanus), and even Philo precedes Antony and Cleopatra, albeit just, onto the stage. Far from standing independent and free, to be judged entirely on their own terms, we know at least something about all these men and women before they appear.

Ibsen too takes care to set up his characters before the audience meets them. The first act of *The Wild Duck* begins with two servants reporting on a dinner taking place next door, involving the play's main characters, and the beginning of *Hedda Gabler* consists of a conversation between the title character's aunt and a servant, in which much is established about Hedda's character (and parentage). The title character doesn't appear at all in the first act of *John Gabriel Borkman*, but is merely heard stomping about upstairs as his wife and her estranged sister renew a long-standing feud. In the opening moments of *Rosmersholm*, Rebecca and Mrs Helseth secretly watch Rosmer's progress towards the house, with Rosmer begining to use the mill path again but still shrinking from going over the bridge. Why? Because 'They cling to their dead a long time at Rosmersholm.'

In comedy, we are told not only about the place of the characters in the plot, but what to look out for. Every major character in Richard Brinsley Sheridan's *The Rivals* is introduced by the servants Fag and Thomas in the opening scene of the play, before any of them appear. The particular characteristic for which Mrs Malaprop is famous (using words 'ingeniously misapplied, without being mispronounced') is noted in that first scene, and reiterated by Julia just before Mrs Malaprop comes in. In George Farquhar's *The Recruiting Officer*, we are told much about the foppish bombast Captain Brazen before his first entrance. By Act 3 Scene 1 we have already heard of a second recruiting officer in Shrewsbury. As Brazen approaches, Justice Balance confesses he doesn't know him, to which Worthy responds:

> But I engage he knows you, and everybody at first sight; his impudence were a prodigy, were not his ignorance proportionable; he has the most universal acquaintance of any man living, for he won't be alone, and nobody will keep him company twice; then he's a Caesar among the women, *veni, vidi, vici,* that's all. If he has but talked with the maid, he swears he has lain with the mistress; but the most surprising part of his character is his memory, which is the most prodigious, and the most trifling in the world.

We thus know what to expect before Brazen makes his entrance, as he duly does, and we enjoy the prediction fulfilled. Farquhar has kept two things back. The first is Brazen's foppishness of manner, which sits engagingly with his military boasting. The second is the precise form in which Brazen demonstrates his supposed 'universal acquaintance', which is the recognisable trope of asking whether a character comes from a particular county branch of a family.

So on hearing of Captain Plume, Brazen inquires whether he is related to Frank Plume in Northamptonshire, but not before he has misunderstood Justice Balance to be called Laconic, and used Brazen's associated memory of 'Poor Jack Laconic', killed at the battle of Landen, to bounce himself into an extended military boast. Once encoded as a character trait, both the familial enquiry and the confusion over Balance's name are reiterated through the play: when the heroine Silvia appears dressed as a man, in the name of Jack Wilful, Brazen's first enquiry is whether he is drawn 'of the Kentish Wilfuls or those of Staffordshire?' The characteristic pays off at the end of the play, when Justice Balance corrects Brazen's mistake about his name. Irrepressible, Brazen insists that he knows Balance's 'whole generation', back to and including 'an uncle that was governor of the Leeward Islands'. The wonder being, of course, that on this one occasion he is absolutely right.

With Brazen, then, an expectation is created, artfully and pleasurably fulfilled, and then put to variable and varied service for the rest of the character's stage life. By contrast, our expositional knowledge of Madame Arkadina in Chekhov's *The Seagull* is partial, suspect, and, when matched with the woman herself, throws as much light on the expositor as the exposited. The young playwright Konstantin has three massive speeches about the great actress before she appears, delivered to his uncle Sorin in response to a question about Sorin's 'sister', so that the young man can assert his view of Arkadina's malice and jealousy before Chekhov need reveal that Konstantin is talking about his own mother.

In his trio of speeches, gently and occasionally interrupted by Sorin, Konstantin berates his mother's self-centredness, emotional carelessness and resentment at her age, relating all of the above to his contempt for the triviality of the contemporary theatre and his desire to create new theatre forms. Thus, Chekhov has invited us to link Konstantin's view of his mother with our view of his play.

When Arkadina arrives, her impatience, languid superiority and not entirely tactful quotations from the play scene in *Hamlet*, appear to confirm everything Konstantin has said about her, and any lingering feeling that the young man doth protest too much is dispelled. However, the fact that the play is indeed awful, and petulantly concluded in mid-sentence by its author (who stomps out, careless of the fact he has left the actress stuck onstage behind the curtain) changes our view of him and thus of her. It's not that Arkadina's response to the play – connecting its pretension with her son's conceit and 'these perpetual jibes at my expense' – is any great departure from what we have been led to expect. But it throws a new and less attractive light on Konstantin, which spills into a more indulgent and understanding view of his mother. So when, within a page of the abrupt ending of the play, Arkadina repents of her sharpness, she becomes a more emotionally interesting and substantial figure thereby.

I've described this set-up in detail because it demonstrates that there is no such thing as an independent character in the theatre; our attitude to a character is created by a matrix of impressions, presented to us in a particular order, and supported by evidence that is also orchestrated. What we think of Hedda Gabler changes moment by moment as we first hear from others about her, and then see her operating with her husband and others, with the others without her husband, and with her husband alone.

Pursuing objectives

If the first principle of character development is to make sure that they are properly introduced, then the second is to show them doing things. As David Mamet puts it:

> When playing poker it is a good idea to determine what cards your opponents might hold. There are two ways to do this. One involves watching their idiosyncrasies – the way they hold their cards when bluffing as opposed to

the way they hold them when they have a strong hand;
their unconscious self-revelatory gestures; the way they
play with their chips when unsure. This method of
gathering information is called looking for 'tells'.

The other way to gather information is to analyze your
opponent's hand according to what he *bets*.

These two methods are analogous – in the Theater – to a
concern with *characterization*, and a concern with
action; or, to put it a bit differently: a concern with the
way a character does something and, on the other hand,
the actual *thing* that he does.[8]

What characters do is pursue objectives, an insight which was
codified by the Russian director Stanislavsky into a theory of
acting which implies a theory of writing. As Chekhov said: tell
me what you want and I'll tell you who you are.

For Stanislavsky and his followers, the way that an actor
reveals these wants is through a series of actions (another and
distinct use of the word), intended to direct other characters
(helpers or opponents) towards the achievement of the first
character's objectives. In his book *Letters to George* – about
directing *The Recruiting Officer* and Timberlake Wertenbaker's
companion piece *Our Country's Good* – Max Stafford-Clark
describes how he and his actors 'action' individual lines with
transitive verbs: in pursuit of the objective, say, of seduction, a
character may befriend, please, intrigue and flatter in as many
lines, to which the other character, in pursuit of the objective of
remaining unseduced, may respond by warning, snubbing, and
challenging before finally spurning.[9]

This is helpful because it demonstrates the third great
principle of character writing: that a characters' objectives are
not necessarily – or even often – pursued directly. They are just
as likely to be pursued by performance and pretence.

Role-play

Actors act characters acting. The great American comedian
George Burns maintained that 'the great thing about acting is
honesty. If you can fake that, then you've got it made.' Or, as
Oscar Wilde insisted, if you give a man a mask, he will tell you

the truth. Among the many things he meant by that is we spend much of our time pursuing genuine objectives through dissemblance of various kinds. It is also true, of course, that we are not entirely in command of this process ourselves. As Eric Bentley puts it:

> In presenting our 'self' to others, we do not have the pleasant and easy choice between a Real Self and a Madison Avenue False Self. There are very many possibilities, and most of us avail ourselves of a considerable number, playing different roles at different times and before different people.[10]

First of all, human beings spend a lot of their lives involved in performative activity. We learn a great deal about the characters in Richard Curtis's *Four Weddings and a Funeral* from their best man speeches and requiem orations. At the start of Peter Nichols' *A Day in the Death of Joe Egg*, the central character is teaching an unruly class; in John Osborne's *The Entertainer*, Archie Rice is entertaining his public, and, in Robert Bolt's *State of Revolution*, a Soviet Minister welcomes the audience as members of the Young Communist League. Although all three men are disguising a great deal, they are not actually *in* disguise; but Rosalind spends most of *As You Like It* – and Viola nearly all of *Twelfth Night* – feigning membership of the opposite sex. Indeed, the turning point of *As You Like It* comes when Rosalind really faints and goes to great lengths to pretend she was pretending. In the quarto text of *King Lear*, Edgar as Poor Tom participates in a mock trial of the woman whose husband has blinded his father; in *Hamlet*, the prince writes a play about the murder of his father by his uncle to perform to his mother; in *Henry IV Part One*, Hal plays himself to Falstaff as his father, in which guise Falstaff insists that Hal banish all his low-life friends except himself.

The playwright Mark Ravenhill makes the point that the right to dress up as someone else has its darker side. In the '60s and '70s, role-play (across class, race and gender) was seen as liberating; now, it's 'just as likely to be seen as entrapping'. Martin Crimp's *Attempts on her Life* is a play about someone entirely defined by other people.[11] Viola and Rosalind are emancipated by their voluntary masquerade; for Hal, Hamlet and Edgar – bad, mad and unclad – the mask appears to have melted into the face.

Performance sometimes (though not always) involves deceit. In Molière's *The Misanthrope* we read Alceste and Oronte's mutual contempt off the excess of their mutual courtesy; in a more complicated way, in Congreve's *The Way of the World*, we understand from Mirabell and Millamant's discussion of their relationship as a commercial contract that in truth their marriage will be nothing of the kind. Similarly, in dialogue, we show that a man is lonely not by having him saying it but by him indulging in what the structuralists call phatic speech, the kind of meandering, often platitudinous dialogue whose primary purpose is to keep the conversation going.

Then there are scenes in which we learn as much about the person we're not hearing as the person we are, and read what's happening inside one person almost entirely from what is said to them by another. A notable example is the scene in Brecht's *Galileo* in which the largely silent Pope is persuaded by the Cardinal Inquisitor to arraign Galileo for blasphemy, as he is ceremonially dressed in his papal robes. There are also characters who surprise us by not turning up: the title character in Jean Anouilh's *Ardèle* appears fleetingly and in silence; the notional central character of *Attempts on her Life* – the 'her' of the title – doesn't appear at all. Other major offstage characters whom we expect to appear (if we haven't read the programme) include Reg in Kevin Elyot's *My Night with Reg*, Ronnie in Arnold Wesker's *Roots*, and Godot.

A converse of the anticipated character who remains absent is the epiphany, the hitherto silent character who speaks. In Stephen Jeffreys' *The Libertine*, a group of Restoration wits gathers to rubbish the poet Dryden's latest play, by the device of attempting, and failing, to find a good bit. As the conversation moves on, a more or less silent prostitute moves upstage with the manuscript and after several minutes announces that she has 'found a good bit' (and she's right). At a key moment in my play *The Shape of the Table*, the hitherto largely instrumental (and almost completely silent) secretary of a group of activists negotiating the end of an East European Communist regime turns on the group she is serving; but as the resigning Communist leaders re-enter the room, her new-found confidence deserts her: 'I'm sorry. I am just the secretary.' There is an anticipation of this device in those figures in Shakespearian comedies who are forced by deceit or magic to reveal the truth of their feelings and desires and are humiliated for it (including Malvolio, Shylock, Parolles and Falstaff).

Role-playing of this order reveals the fourth principle of character creation. In drama we are not seeing ordinary people engaging in the regular business of everyday life, which is, of course, the habitual. We are seeing people in exceptional circumstances, and thus we are seeing them behaving uncharacteristically. As George Eliot says in *Middlemarch*, 'Unwonted circumstances may make us all rather unlike ourselves.' The fact that drama happens when we behave surprisingly is the reason why the playwright Terry Johnson advises playwrights to give every character a surprising characteristic. It's a trick, but it reflects a truth, which is that few individuals are dealt an entirely congruent hand, and it is exceptional situations which reveal this fact to us. When, in writing *Insignificance*, Johnson first had the idea of Marilyn Monroe explaining the theory of relativity with the aid of a flashlight, a model of Charlie Chaplin and two small toy trains, it was integral to his conceit that the person she was explaining it to was Albert Einstein. It would be something of an understatement to say that this is a scene in which both people behave uncharacteristically.

So the fourth principle is that, as effective characters pursue objectives and confront obstacles, one or other should be pursued or confronted for the first time. The detective may have pursued the objective of unmasking the murderer a hundred times, but the cunning author will see to it that each new case presents a new obstacle. The experienced spy may confront his usual enemy in an unusual guise. In the rake's progress – from *Don Juan* to Arthur Schnitzler's *La Ronde* to Bill Naughton's *Alfie* – the skill is to ring the changes on each seduction, altering either the seducer's objective or the nature of the seducee's response.

Characteristics

However, there are characters who for reasons either of their position in the story, their limitations as human beings, or the ramrod strength of their personalities, clearly *do* behave characteristically most of the time. Even here, it is the character's objective which animates the characteristic, not the other way round. Both Dogberry and Mrs Malaprop herself confuse vocabulary in a doomed attempt to impress. In Peter Shaffer's *Amadeus*, the Emperor has a running phrase ('there it is') which is surprisingly amusing in performance, for the simple reason that it is delivered by the only person present with the power to change the circumstances which the phrase purports to cast as fate. While in Stephen Bill's *Curtains*, a character's incapacity to finish a sentence takes flight as a device when the sentences – many of them about the problem of how to conceal the embarrassing fact of his mother's murder – are easy to finish (and are, by us).

In writing *Pentecost*, I came up against a problem most writers come up against from time to time. I had a character function without a character: a Catholic priest, one of several people who seek to claim ownership of an abandoned East European church in which a possibly priceless medieval fresco has been found. In the second act, the priest becomes involved in the climax of a siege drama after the church and its then inhabitants have been taken hostage by a group of asylum-seekers. In the first act, he was part of a double act with an Orthodox priest, having been – and this was part of the problem – initially conceived as one of a trio of priests, representing the Catholic, Orthodox and Uniate confessions. Abandoning the Uniate priest meant in essence that I was combining his character function with the Catholic. While I found, I think, a good character for the Orthodox priest, the irreconcilable aspects of the combined second and third priest left me with a character who wasn't anything beyond a role.

I wanted to find a characteristic which would perform three functions: it would express a backstory, it would provide a contrast with the Orthodox priest, and it would develop interestingly and dramatically when the priest is under pressure as he seeks to prevent the hostage crisis going critical at the end of the play. This meant that the characteristic couldn't be an obsession with baseball or flirting with girls. In fact, it ended up being a kind of verbal tic. I decided that in order to contrast with the Orthodox priest, the Catholic should be a returning exile whose father had taken him to England at the age of twelve. This would mean that his English would be good, but would still have the odd mannerism that set him apart from a native English speaker.

One of the things we all do when speaking in foreign languages is use favourite phrases or figures slightly more often than a native (indeed, I had the Orthodox priest, whose English is obviously much more limited, frequently use the phrase 'I must say' as an emphatic). With the Catholic's much firmer grip, I didn't want his tic to be a single phrase, but really a rhetorical formation, which would distinguish him from his older, more extrovert, innocent and immediately emotional religious rival. What I came up with was the old politician's trick of presuming that the argument you are putting forward must be generally agreed by all right-thinking persons ('as is surely universally accepted...'). Such a tic would make my priest sound precise, the careful changes he would ring on the figure would demonstrate his considered use of his second language, and if used under circumstances of high tension and drama the device would remain workable but would tend to vex those for whom what he had to say was far from self-evident. I then made a list of such phrases, which I had at my side when writing his scenes, most of which I worked in: 'naturally', 'of course', 'as is generally agreed', 'as Father Bojovic is well aware', 'as the whole world knows', 'as is surely clear to everyone', 'as must be obvious to everyone', 'as everyone knows', 'as it is well understood today', 'as you must acknowledge', 'as you must surely understand'. This last phrase was used at a crisis point in the hostage drama, and was flung back in his face by the hostage-taker's leader, one of whose own characteristics was to take other people's phrases and turn them back against them. So I was able to dovetail two characteristics at a moment when it would serve the drama.

There are actors who say that the first thing they get is the walk or even the set of the shoulders. Writers can also start with the mannerism and move inwards, but only if that mannerism can be put under threat, tested, be thrown into relief and/or fall apart at the character's moment of crisis.

Monomaniacs

Then there are those characters whose pursuit of their objective is so single-minded, whose performance is so sure and whose characteristics so constrained by their desires, that their opponents are not treated as people, but turned into things. In psychoanalytical terms, we are talking of monomaniacs. In both comedy and tragedy, such a person is at least one example of what Ben Jonson defines (in the induction to *Every Man Out of His Humour*) in the following terms:

> As when some one peculiar quality
> Doth so possess a man, that it doth draw
> All his affects, his spirits, and his powers,
> In their confluctions, all to run one way.
> This may be truly said to be a humour.

Although formulated as an observation of a certain sort of human being, Jonson's 'humour' is also, and perhaps primarily, a method. That's certainly how two modern writers approach character development: the novelist Martin Amis likes to take two elements of his own personality and imagine what he'd be like if that were all there was; John Cleese says that every comic actor's greatest creation is what they'd be like if they didn't have a sense of humour.

The fact that both Cleese and Amis express negatively what Jonson expresses positively seems to me to demonstrate the essential truth of the monomaniac in dramatic art (and I'd argue in life): that he (or she, from Aeschylus's Clytemnestra via the Queen Margaret of the Wars of the Roses plays to Beverley in Mike Leigh's *Abigail's Party*) is not only in thrall to overwhelming determinations but also in contest with something lost. Tirso de Molina's Don Juan announces himself as the man without a name; Faust's Mephistopheles confesses: 'I am that spirit which endlessly denies'; both Mr Hyde and Dr Jekyll are, after all, only half a person. At the end of *Richard III*, seeing the ghosts of his victims and realising they are the manifestations of his conscience, Richard attempts to cut off those parts of himself (his guilt and his fear, even his self-love) which threaten his determination to defeat his enemies. What might look like the thin characterisation of monomaniacal characters is in fact the acknowledgement of the truth that we build ourselves by exclusion as much as inclusion. In his autobiography, Peter Brook describes an exercise by the Polish director Jerzy Grotowski, in which actors are invited to imitate the type of person they most detest. What they reveal, of course, is their own deepest nature.[12]

As Cambridge philosopher Mary Midgley argues in her incomparable 1984 essay on *Wickedness*, evil is not so much a present force as an absence. Goodness is the capacity to employ our impulses for purposes beyond our own immediate gratification; evil is a lack of the capacity to be whole. One obvious example of this lack is a want of empathy: people do evil to people when they fail to see the world through their victims' eyes. And indeed, the narrower our view of the world, the more it shrinks to our own wants and needs, the emptier we become. 'Happy to sacrifice the whole integrity of his being for the sake of his spotless reputation,' Midgley writes of Stevenson's protagonist, 'Jekyll has not so much "become two people" as ceased to be anybody. He has become hollow, losing his centre, from refusing to acknowledge his shadow side.'[13] This is true of all villains, from Iago to Milton's Satan, and for a simple reason:

> Obsession has to carry with it the atrophy and gradual death of all faculties not involved in whatever may be the obsessing occupation. And among those faculties is the power of caring for others, insofar as they are not the objects of obsession.[14]

People argue that Iago isn't a real character because he displays such a single-minded obsession with achieving his goal; on the other hand, Eric Bentley says the character fascinates not because we all know an Iago, but because there's some of Iago in all of us. That's certainly true: but I fear we may know more Iagos than we think. After all, nobody starts out as Iago.

In both *The Godfather* and *The Godfather: Part II*, a full and rounded young man turns into a monomaniac. In the first film, it is Michael, who attempts to evade his family fate by escaping into the Sicilian countryside: his destiny catches up with him and drags him back. In the second, we are reminded of what Michael has lost by the flashbacks into his father's past, and his father's initiation into the brutal rites of revenge. So each is a reminder of the other's loss, of innocence, youth, childhood, of the world *outside*. It is, of course, no coincidence that Marlon Brando's Don Corleone dies playing with a child in a garden; as indeed the child who is to become that other great movie gangster, Citizen Kane, is called indoors from his sled on the journey that will lead him to his lonely death in Xanadu. In fact, the entire dramatic structure of Herman J. Mankiewicz and Orson Welles's *Citizen Kane* is designed to express its action: 'A man who sets out to achieve an end, achieves it, but discovers too late that it wasn't what he wanted after all.' The quest of the movie is to discover the meaning of Kane's final word, 'Rosebud', which turns out to be the name of the sled that was taken from him as a boy. Dime-store psychiatry, as a screenwriter put it, but it makes for one of the most powerful endings in cinema.

It always seems odd that those who see drama as characters pursing objectives pay so little attention to the obvious question: whether or not those objectives are achieved. Terry Johnson thinks that this is a foregone conclusion: his definition of drama is the discovery of 'what people want and why they can't have it'. As we've seen, this perception is at its starkest in gangster stories, at the end of which the protagonist discovers that he never really wanted what he strove so hard – and at such a cost – to achieve. This is, of course, the fate of the monomaniac, and it is at that moment when the individual character emerges from the role. Once again, it is the moment of reversal, when the character realises or understands the true nature and limit of the role into which their own ambition or outward circumstance has propelled them.

Rank, office, relation, role and character

The persons we meet in plays can be categorised in a number of ways. They may serve in an office (ruler, commander, priest) which may imply a rank (king, general, bishop). They have relationships with other characters (wife, son, daughter; employer, subordinate). Some relationships imply an office and/or a rank (servant, butler). People also have a role in the play, as hero, villain, victim or helper. Sometimes that role has melded with its associated characteristics and become an archetype (which is, after all, a stereotype which has stuck). And then they have a character.

We've seen that, for the neoclassicists, these categories should make a perfect fit. In *Don Quixote*, Cervantes complains of plays which defy verisimilitude by showing 'an old man who's courageous and a young one who's a coward, a lackey who's a great orator, a page who's a counsellor, a king who's a porter and a princess who's a cleaning woman'.[15] In great drama, however, a perfect fit is the last thing you want. The writer Clive James identifies what he calls the 'jobswap' principle of great comedy: the simple technique of inserting a character into a profession for which they are temperamentally unsuited. Dogberry is not a good judge, and David Brent is a terrible office manager; Basil Fawlty might do many things well, but he shouldn't be running a hotel.

This principle applies far beyond comedy. As Eric Bentley says of Othello: 'He has the wrong virtues for the particular situation, and the wrong weaknesses.'[16] Richard III is a great killer and Coriolanus a great soldier, but both are terrible leaders (albeit in different ways). Hamlet is suited to neither his role as avenger nor his office as prince, though he would spot Iago's duplicity at the start (as Richard III would dispose of Claudius before the end of Act 1). In *Three Sisters*, Andrei is head of the Prozorov family and his role is to rescue the family from their provincial torpor by returning them to Moscow; but, failing to gain the rank necessary to fulfil that task, he shows himself temperamentally suited to neither his office nor his role. In *Mrs Warren's Profession*, Shaw wants us to believe that Vivie Warren, who has defied her womanly office by getting a job, and her rank by refusing to marry, will at least fulfil her daughterly role and forgive her mother at the end. In fact, she abandons her, and something else happens instead.

What happens to Vivie Warren is that, by defying our expectations, she turns from a role into a character. The reverse can happen: you could say that the metamorphoses of the Pope in *Galileo* and of Hal in *Henry IV, Part Two* consist of two fully fledged characters, promoted in rank, accepting the limitations of their new roles. And there is an argument that, as a writer, Shakespeare undertook that journey himself, as Othello thinned into Leontes, Rosalind into Imogen and Puck into Ariel. Some characters begin and remain as roles: you could define melodrama as a genre in which role, office and character completely accord: the hero behaves entirely heroically, the prince royally, the servant obsequiously (or loyally), the villain villainously, and the victim only emerges from a deep swoon to thank her rescuer at the end.

But in great drama, the most memorable and indeed the most meaningful moment is when the character departs from and even challenges his or her role; when the old man is brave, the lackey eloquent, the page gives sage advice, and the cleaner behaves like a princess (or, indeed, the other way round). It is the character – unpredictable, irrepressible – who declares unilateral independence from the tyranny of the preordained. This act of revolt was well described by soap actor Tamzin Outhwaite, setting out her stall for her Mel in *EastEnders*: 'I didn't want her turning into a wimpy character like so many women in soaps. You know, they're either bitches or they're slags or they're victims. I wanted to give Mel a bit of everything so that she would be three-dimensional.'[17] Three-dimensional, in the sense that her character would outstrip her role.

Often, characters rebel against their role in the drama by rejecting its associated responsibilities (the soldier who deserts his army, the king who abdicates his throne, the politician who abandons his prewritten text). Sometimes it seems that the character has rebelled against the play: both Falstaff and Brecht's Mother Courage seem larger than the plots which contain them. And although, as stated, character is revealed to us through the emplotment rules of drama, it is in many ways its wild card, the element which breaks through the limitations of the play's predictable project, providing the surprising reversal which makes each individual play unique. If the persons in their office, role and rank undertake the predictable project of the play, then the character, in all its wayward individuality, provides the unexpected reversal. And it's at the moment of the character's rebellion, the moment of the 'but', that the stereotype transforms into a character.

In many cases, the person keeps the role, but becomes a character *as well*. But sometimes the character strips off the role and stands for the first time as an individual, clothed only in their independence. In a radio interview, the playwright David Rudkin described how people assemble mental houses to live in, consisting of attitudes, clichés, passions, prophecies, myths and rituals, tokens, totems and taboos which add up to 'an apparatus of identity'. The pattern which recurs in Rudkin's work is the process whereby that apparatus of identity is broken away:

> The characters learn that what makes them true, what makes them who they are, is not – as they thought – those tokens by which they belong, those tokens that make them brothers and members of their community, or their tribe or their people or their world. What makes them what they are is precisely those attributes that make strangers of them, that makes exiles and transgressors of them. So that, at the end of the drama, the characters are left naked and alone and at a beginning.[18]

1. Quoted in Marvin Carlson, *Theories of the Theatre*, Ithaca, New York: Cornell University Press, 1984, pp. 25-6.

2. *Ibid.* p. 79.

3. Aristotle, 'Poetics' in *Classical Literary Criticism*, trans. T.S. Dorsch, London and New York: Penguin, 1965, p. 51.

4. John Lennard and Mary Luckhurst, *The Drama Handbook: A Guide to Reading Plays*, Oxford: Oxford University Press, 2002, pp. 78-9.

5. Tami D. Cowden, Caro LaFever and Sue Viders, *The Complete Writer's Guide to Heroes and Heroines*, Hollywood: Lone Eagle Publishing Company, 2000.

6. Quoted in Eric Bentley, *The Life of the Drama*, London: Methuen, 1965, p. 56.

7. *Ibid.* p. 55.

8. David Mamet, *Writing in Restaurants*, London and New York: Penguin, 1986, p. 118.

9. Max Stafford-Clark, *Letters to George*, London: Nick Hern Books, 1989, pp. 66-70.

10. Eric Bentley, *op. cit.*, p. 188.

11. Mark Ravenhill, 'A World of Spectacle', *The Guardian*, 20 October 2007.

12. Peter Brook, *Threads of Time*, London: Methuen, 1998, p. 170.

13. Mary Midgley, *Wickedness*, London: Routledge, 2001, pp. 125, 136.

14. *Ibid.* p. 160.

15. Miguel de Cervantes Saavedra, *Don Quixote*, trans. John Rutherford, London and New York: Penguin, 2004, p. 444.

16. Eric Bentley, *op. cit.*, p. 268.

17. In *OK!*, quoted in *The Guardian*, 22 March 2001.

18. Interview by Patrick Wright, *Outriders*, BBC Radio 3, 4 February 1999.

4
Genre

Genre

'Action' is not the only dramaturgical term with a multiplicity of contradictory meanings. 'Form' is as problematic a concept in drama as anywhere else. If you use the word 'genre' in its common and (frankly) most helpful sense, you find yourself up against Plato, Aristotle and the BBC. Because different categorisations reshuffle the whole pack (for the BBC, drama itself is a genre), it's necessary to work your way down through the hierarchy. The following lexicon seems to me the clearest and most useful.

Categories

Works of fiction are written for a **medium**. These include the **book**, with its numbered pages, chapters, other forms of division (including paragraphs), punctuative conventions like quotation, content listing and various kinds of section identification and naming, illustrations, author's biography, prefaces, forewords, introductions, acknowledgements, indexes, bibliographies, and covers (with their flyleaves, endpapers, dustjackets, illustrations and blurbs).

The elements of **cinema** include its present audience but absent performers, titles and credits, subtitles, camera movements (long shots, close-ups, pans, tracking), editing devices (cuts, mixes, superimpositions, splitscreens and fades), special effects, colouration, scenes and sequences. **Television** shares many of the technical elements of cinema, and the institutional and presentational structures of **radio** (channels, programmes, listings, titles, credits, commercial and preview breaks). Radio is further defined by its limitations: it is easy to convey approaching and receding, harder (because of variable reception quality) to guarantee that listeners will read side to side, impossible to convey (as such) people moving up and down.

Finally there is the **stage**, with its present performers and (usually) still and silent audience; its acts and intervals, scene changes and curtain calls; its posters, programmes and playtexts. Among the most durable conventions of the medium are the presumptive existence of the fourth wall between the actors and the audience, and those devices – the aside and the soliloquy – which permit communication through it.

Within those media, there are a number of largely but not entirely media-specific **forms**. Historically, the stage has been dominated by **theatre**, **opera** and **ballet**; elements of all of which are retained in newer stage forms like the **musical**, **pantomime**, **cabaret**, **circus**, **variety**, **burlesque** and **vaudeville**. Print fiction appears in the form of the **novel** (including, now, the **graphic novel**), the **novella**, the **short story**, and the **narrative poem**, largely in books but also in magazines. In our age, fictional storytelling in cinema is dominated by the **feature film**.

Although there are danced and sung dramas, and indeed readings, in the broadcast media, television and radio fiction is dominated by three forms. First, the **single play**, initially evoking the stage play but now much more specific to the demands and opportunities of radio and, in television, the vocabulary of the feature film. Then there are the two forms which first radio and then television borrowed from magazine publication and made their own: the continuous **serial**, which tells the developing stories of a mutating group of characters within a particular milieu; and the drama or comedy **series**, in which a largely consistent group of characters confront different (though often comparable) situations in separate and coherent episodes. Most drama series now contain both series and serial elements, with each episode telling one or more complete stories against the background of the developing lives of the regular characters, the mechanism codified in Steve Bochco's *LA Law* for NBC, and Jeremy Brock and Paul Unwin's *Casualty* for the BBC.

In addition to these scheduling particularities, many radio and most television dramas also tell a recognisable kind of story, most usually – and usefully – described as a genre.

Defining genre

There are two traditional ways of looking at genre which are interesting, but neither of them are hugely helpful to the playwright today. The first is the Aristotelian (and Platonic) definition of genre in terms of the form of enunciation, distinguishing between **diagesis** (the writer's authorial voice) and **mimesis** (speaking through characters). Oddly enough, as theatre has moved away from realism and started raiding the novel for different narrative forms, the question of enunciation has become more relevant: you could argue that a play written in the author's narrative voice, like David Hare's one-person, self-performed *Via Dolorosa*, is essentially diagetic, as are those verbatim plays which employ direct quotation.

The second traditional definition sees genre as a function of the status of the characters. As I pointed out in the chapter on Character, Roman critics described a play with highly placed characters as a tragedy, one with low-life characters as a comedy, and a play with a mix of both as a tragicomedy.

Much more useful for playwrights is the idea of genre as a set of expectations of storyline, character, locale and outcome. Any discussion of genre exposes theatre's dirty little secret, which is that audiences know the ending of most plays (or certainly the *sort* of ending) before they begin. The structuralist critic Jonathan Culler defines genres as 'sets of conventions and expectations', noting that 'whether we are reading a detective story or a romance, a lyric poem or a tragedy, we are on the lookout for different things and make assumptions about what will be significant'.[1]

In other words, genre is the possession not of the writer but of the audience. It is possible to define a genre by listing its regular narrative elements, but many of the most noted examples of particular genres may drop one or another: Agatha Christie abandoned Hercule Poirot's loyal if dim-witted sidekick, Captain Hastings, early on in her whodunnit career, and not all Westerns are set in one-horse towns with a saloon. But, as John Lennard and Mary Luckhurst put it, 'The point is not that "All Westerns are like *this*", but that the *idea* of Westerns links these various elements so any one of them leads a reader/viewer to *expect* some of the others – an expectation that may be fulfilled or disappointed.'[2] So, the knowledge that a work is written within a particular genre leads us to look out for, or to recognise, expected elements. If the sidekick does say something insightful, we are attuned to recognise it, and to wait (as we usually have to) for the detective to reveal how it fits into the patterns of his or her own thinking. We are also able to spot unusual casting, as when a particular expected role is taken by someone with an unexpected office or rank. In the first of Lynda La Plante's *Prime Suspect* series, the sidekick who gave DCI Jane Tennison her crucial insight was a hitherto minor, junior, and female member of the male-dominated team.

Genre expectations also imply certain readings of events. As Terence Hawkes argues, genre enables the reader 'to *decode* literature in the same mode as it was *encoded* by the writer'.[3] If we know that the crime we are watching or reading about is part of a whodunnit we will ask different questions than those we ask watching *Agamemnon* or reading *Bleak House* or *Dracula*. For example:

A woman walks along a hotel landing, unlocks a door and enters her room, where she finds a man lying on the floor with his throat cut. She hears a sound and rushes out of the room to see the back of a person disappearing quickly down the stairs.

Then one of three things happen:

She calls the police who commit a Chief Inspector and his Sergeant to investigate the crime.

Or:

The person descending the stairs leaves the building, gets into a car and nods to his driver, who turns the corner before a third person sits up in the back seat and shoots him.

Or:

Hearing the woman's call, the person descending the stairs turns back. It is the man she saw dead in the room a moment before.

The first scenario suggests the classic whodunnit, in which we are invited to read the death as a puzzle which it will be the principal purpose of the plotting to complicate and then to solve. The second model is a crime thriller, in which we know the identity of the criminal but we are invited to follow the twists and turns of the pursuit. The third is clearly a story of the supernatural.

However, the point of genre is not only that we can read what will happen off what has happened, but that we can close off options even before the story has begun. Let us say for example that the second scenario (the person shot in the car) happens in what we know to be a whodunnit: we can be pretty sure that whatever else he may have done, the person on the stairs didn't kill the man in the woman's room. Similarly, if the third scenario occurred not in a ghost story but in either a whodunnit or a thriller, we'd be safe in assuming that there'd turn out to be a perfectly rational explanation for our seeing the murdered man alive, well and proceeding in a downwardly direction towards the street.

In other words, our presumptions about the death are informed by our presumptions about the genre. A thriller death can be random, but a whodunnit death can't. The thriller or whodunnit reader would feel cheated if a death turned out to have supernatural causes. Genres are distinguished by how they are read as much as by how they are written, and this applies as much to the traditional genres as to the genres of our own time.

Traditional genres

Contrast and convergence

Traditional criticism emphasises the differences between comedy and tragedy, the two genres that dominated drama up until the end of the nineteenth century. The fourth-century critic Evanthius defines them in starkly contrasting terms:

> In comedy the fortunes of men are middle-class, the dangers are slight, and the ends of the action are happy; but in tragedy everything is the opposite – the characters are great men, the fears are intense, and the ends

> disastrous. In comedy the beginning is troubled, the end
> tranquil; in tragedy the events follow the reverse order.
> And in tragedy the kind of life is shown that is to be
> shunned; while in comedy the kind is shown that is to be
> sought after. Finally, in comedy the story is always
> fictitious; while tragedy is often based on historical truth.[4]

However glaring the divergence between them, Evanthius gives equal weight to the two genres, while making the obvious point that – faced with the choice – we'd all prefer the Forest of Arden to the House of Atreus. Other critics have emphasised the less profound – and less appealing – aspects of the comic world. In the tenth-century fragment the *Tractatus Coislinianus* (which some literary historians think to be part of Aristotle's lost work on comedy), comedy is defined as 'an imitation of an action that is ludicrous and imperfect'[5] (in contrast to Aristotle's tragic action, 'worth serious attention, complete in itself, and of some amplitude'). Both Ben Jonson and Oliver Goldsmith memorably attribute the charm of comedy to the fact that the audience feels itself superior both to the characters and their circumstances: for Goldsmith, 'comedy should excite our laughter by ridiculously exhibiting the Follies of the Lower Part of Mankind';[6] for Jonson in the prologue to *Every Man in His Humour*, comedy's task is to 'sport with human follies, not with crimes'. As Eric Bentley points out, the fact that we look up at tragedy and down on comedy allows us to displace our guilt onto comic characters; while tragedy 'entails perhaps the most direct, single-minded, and complete identification with guilt that is offered by any art whatsover'.[7]

What is striking about all of these definitions is that they define one or both of the genres in terms of the other. These writers are not alone in doing this. The Restoration dramatist William Wycherley insisted that the comedy of tragedy was that it ends in death, and the tragedy of comedy that it ends in marriage. For Oscar Wilde, the comedy of life was that 'the soul is born old, but grows young', while tragedy arose from the fact that the body does the opposite.[8] Alan Ayckbourn defines comedy as unfinished tragedy; Woody Allen as 'tragedy plus time'. For Orson Welles, a happy ending means the story isn't over; for the literary critic Northrop Frye, by contrast, 'the sense of tragedy as a prelude to comedy seems almost inseparable from anything explicitly Christian'.⁹ All these definitions imply that both author and audience are aware during both comedies and tragedies that things could go the other way.

This convergence between the two genres accounts for the sense we so often have of one aping the other. If Shakespeare's tragedies are unsuitably and notoriously overpopulated with clowns, then his comedies are unexpectedly bloody: of the fourteen folio comedies, five contain actual deaths, five the serious threat of death to a central character or characters, four a central character in mourning, three a war before or during the action, and no less than eight an apparent death which turns out to be counterfeited or assumed.

This insertion of tragic elements into comedies is particularly striking in Shakespeare's problem plays *Measure for Measure* and *All's Well That Ends Well*. Both plays are clearly comedies (*All's Well* has an averted death, an assumed death, a disguised heroine, and a bed swap). However, they challenge traditional comic meanings by a subtle reworking of expected elements. Both plays end with marriages, but of an unsatisfactory character: in *All's Well*, Bertram is forced into a marriage he's spent the play resisting, and only one of the four marriages arranged at the end of *Measure* is a love-match (two are imposed on reluctant bridegrooms, while the Duke's proposal to Isabella is not accepted). Far from entering Shakespeare's habitual Arcadian green world, the fourth act of *Measure for Measure* takes place in a prison, on death row.

The equivalent scenes of *All's Well That Ends Well* take place in an army camp, in which a character is duped into thinking he's about to be executed. That character, Parolles, is essentially a boastful soldier, and thus drawn from the same Plautine tradition as Falstaff and Pistol. But unlike them, or any other of the characters denied a happy ending in the comedies, he acquires self-knowledge. Overhearing Parolles plan his pretence at heroism, Lord Dumaine asks, 'Is it possible he should know what he is, and be that he is?' After he is exposed and humiliated, Parolles answers that question in the affirmative:

> Captain I'll be no more,
> But I will eat and drink and sleep as soft
> As captain shall. Simply the thing I am

Shall make me live. Who knows himself a braggart,
Let him fear this, for it will come to pass
That every braggart shall be found an ass.

The hybrid nature of *Romeo and Juliet* – which really is a comedy gone wrong – is demonstrated by a variant of this comic hallmark (Juliet's pretend death) which turns through tragic accident into a real one. Similarly, the play starts unhappily, with a feud that has uncanny echoes of the early acts of *The Merchant of Venice*: echoes that include a gang of rough boys, a charismatic leader of the pack (Gratiano=Mercutio), a melancholy outsider (Antonio=Romeo), an intertribal romance, a carnival and a balcony scene. While later on (in *Romeo and Juliet*), a marriage turns into a funeral, anticipating both *Much Ado About Nothing* and *Antony and Cleopatra* ('I will be / A bridegroom in my death, and run into't / As to a lover's bed'). At the beginning of *Hamlet*, the procedure is reversed ('The funeral baked meats / Did coldly furnish forth the marriage tables'), as it is in Middleton and Rowley's *A New Way to Please You*, in which 'the same rosemary that serves for the funeral shall serve for the wedding'.

The common plot

Like a sonic scan, these echoes reveal the shared topography beneath. The event that initiates the dramatic action of both classical comedy and tragedy is likely to be an act of social disruption. In tragedy it's usually a crime, or, more particularly, an act of usurpation. Comic plots can be instigated by a usurpation too (as happens in both *The Tempest* and *As You Like It*), but a remarkable number start with the imposition of a bad law, whether that be the law which allows Antonio and Shylock's bond in *The Merchant of Venice*, makes fornication a capital offence in *Measure for Measure*'s Vienna, forces Hermia to marry Demetrius on pain of death in *A Midsummer Night's Dream*, or prevents Bianca marrying until Katherine is betrothed in *The Taming of the Shrew*. Alternatively, the play may start with an act of imposture, whether it be the enforced disguising of Viola or Rosalind, or the more calculated imposture in Jonson's *The Alchemist*, Farquhar's *The Beaux Stratagem*, Sheridan's *The Rivals*, Goldsmith's *She Stoops to Conquer* or Wilde's *The Importance of Being Earnest*. Similarly, Oedipus is an impostor who usurps a throne; Antigone is the victim of the imposition of an unjust law.

This initial disruption involves some kind of breach of faith, or broken contract. A striking number of tragic actions involve someone promising that something will happen which then doesn't, or promising that they will do something and then not delivering, by deliberation or otherwise. Coriolanus promises to save Rome, Iago to tell Othello the truth, Goneril and Regan that they love Lear, Hamlet that he will avenge his father's murder. Oedipus does keep his promise to save Thebes, to terrible effect on himself and his family; and Marlowe's Doctor Faustus – though not Goethe's Faust – has to keep the promise to give up his soul to Mephistopheles.

The comic variant of the broken promise is ineffective disguise. This can be literal, but more often we're talking of the failure of pretence, the fact that ultimately the truth will out, the hypocrite will be exposed (Malvolio, Volpone), the true love object will be revealed (Rosalind, Hermia), the servant pretending to be master will be unmasked (in *The Alchemist* and, later, Nikolai Gogol's *The Government Inspector*), the slummer-down will be exposed (*She Stoops to Conquer*), the ruler pretending to be an outcast will reveal himself (*Measure for Measure*, Hal in both *Henry IV* and *Henry V*).

What people know

What broken promises and ineffective disguises share is differential knowledge, the root of dramatic or proleptic irony (dramatic, when the audience knows something but a significant character doesn't; proleptic, when none of the characters knows what's going on, as in plays we know are going backwards or are branded 'tragedy'). So, we know Iago is lying, Rosalind's a girl. We know when Hal tells Falstaff he will reject him he's telling us the truth, because he's told us so (but no one else). In Act 4 of *King Lear*, the mad Lear doesn't know who Gloucester is. Gloucester knows Lear's identity, but not his son's, because he can't see. In the fifth act, we know Cordelia's been condemned to death when no one else does (except for Edmund). In Edmond Rostand's *Cyrano de Bergerac* we know that the unattractive but poetic Cyrano is writing the lovely but tongue-tied Christian's letters for him to the beautiful Roxanne. In *The Importance of Being Earnest*, when Jack arrives at his country home mourning his wicked brother Ernest, we know that Ernest is in fact an invention. Jack knows this too, but he doesn't know that his friend Algernon is presently in the same house, pretending to be the same brother. We know that, but we don't yet know that Algernon really is Jack's brother, and Jack really is called Ernest. We know that Jack and Algernon will marry Gwendolen and Cecily, because we know the play's a comedy.

The importance of what people know when – what the screenwriter Michael Eaton calls the 'choreography of knowledge' – is obvious in classical tragedy, though it's worth noting how brilliantly Sophocles choreographs the information available to the Messenger, Oedipus, Jocasta and us (things are organised so that the Messenger can reveal what he assumes to be welcome intelligence – that Oedipus is not the son of Polybus – at precisely the moment when we've gathered sufficient information to know that this is the worst possible news). The release of information in the correct order is the fundamental skill of the whodunnit. But the ordered revelation of knowledge is also central to the art of realist writers like Ibsen. Indeed, the difference between what we know and what the characters know is not just a mechanism for the unfolding of plot but also the expression of the play's fundamental meaning.

So, in the second act of *Ghosts*, Oswald Alving tells his mother that he has developed what is obviously syphilis, which he has either caught himself or inherited from his deceased father. He wants to believe the latter, but he knows from his mother's letters that his father was a man of singular uprightness and virtue, and so it's his own fault that his life is ruined. Now, we in the audience know that Mrs Alving lied in her letters, that Captain Alving was a drunk, a womaniser and a reprobate, and that if she told Oswald this, he'd know it wasn't his fault after all. The scene thus forces our attention onto the two questions that Ibsen wants us to ask: why Oswald doesn't want to believe that his father was to blame for his disease, and why Mrs Alving won't tell him that he was. The answers to these questions – two different but corrodingly complementary varieties of socially induced guilt – contain the meaning of the play.

Irony is often seen as a dispensible extra; as the novelist Julian Barnes imagines a Hollywood producer remarking, 'Irony is what people miss.' In fact, it is the essential spring of the drama. What happens in *Ghosts* is an example of what J.L. Styan calls that 'steady and insistent communication to the privileged spectator of a meaning hidden from the characters' through which dramatists do most of their work. Once again, irony is not merely a plotting contrivance or a stylistic device, but *'a way of seeing'*, no less than 'drama's essential tool'.[10]

The liminal zone

Most importantly, comedy and tragedy share a space in which the lies are exposed, the disguises are tested, and the truth of who people are is ultimately revealed. That this space is so often out of doors – the countryside, the magic island or forest, the military camp, the field of battle, the blasted heath, the graveyard – is beyond coincidence.

In Shakespeare's Arcadian comedies, the characters start in the court, enter the green world, and return to the court, albeit changed, at the end. Sometimes – as in *As You Like It* – the return to court is projected, after the end of the play's stage time. In a generically hybrid play like *Romeo and Juliet*, the outside appears in a comic and a tragic guise: Friar Lawrence's cell is where the lovers make the impossible become possible, planning and making their marriage; Romeo takes the decision to die on the plague-ridden streets of Mantua. In the great tragedies, Lear and Timon stalk from the castle and the city on to the blasted heath. But sometimes the tragic protagonist refuses to leave the security of his city, court or castle, and the countryside has to come in and get him: the symbolic meaning both of the ghosts of Richard III's victims traversing the field of battle between Richard and Richmond's tents, and, in *Macbeth*, of Birnam Wood coming to Dunsinane.

In exploring the relationship of location to genre, there are two special cases, one a tragedy, one usually seen as a comedy (though also defined as a romance). There isn't a heath in *Hamlet*; its protagonist dies indoors. But all the crucial developments happen outside: Hamlet learns the truth about his father's death on the battlements; he takes the decision to return and kill Claudius on the plain across which Fortinbras has marched his army; his great meditation on the democracy of death occurs outside, in the graveyard; and, after his death, his body will be borne back up to the battlements to lie in state. Further, the imagery of Hamlet's madness blows in from the open air. Ophelia's first report of Hamlet's distemper ends with him stumbling 'out o'doors'; his and Polonius's elliptical discussion of the shape of clouds takes place in a room, at night.

The whole of *The Tempest* takes place outside, on a magic island: Prospero was usurped many years before the beginning of the play, and his return to his dukedom follows its end. Otherwise, seemingly, the play follows the traditional Arcadian pattern, with its presumed deaths, comic interludes and closing romance. However, there are three significant elements in the ending which suggest that Shakespeare was inviting the audience to take a more sombre view. First, its protagonist is a single, elderly widower, rather than a pair of young lovers (as if Jaques was the protagonist of *As You Like It*). Second, Prospero's abjuration of his 'rough magic' involves breaking a staff, burying a book, and plucking off a cloak, in an echo of the stripping of old men in *Timon of Athens* and *King Lear*. Third, the powers that Prospero abjures include the resurrection of the dead ('graves at my command / Have waked their sleepers, oped, and let 'em forth'), and he insists that, once restored to his Milanese Dukedom, 'every third thought shall be my grave'. Prospero's announcement that 'our revels now are ended' is often taken to be Shakespeare's resignation speech; but it is also his characters' farewell to a comic world of magic, romantic bliss and eternal life, and their return to a real and tragic world in which some of us may marry but all of us will die.

Whether literally or metaphorically, then, Shakespeare sites the two great rites of passage of our lives, between childhood and adulthood and between life and death, in the open air. The first story ends with ceremony, the second with its abandonment. Indeed, you might define Shakespeare's two principal genres in starkly simple terms: in the comedies, people are driven into the countryside where they dress up as other people, come in again, and get married; in the tragedies, they strip off, stay outside, and die.

Continuing echoes

The idea of the outside as a special, magic place has anthropological justification. In his *Essays on Performance Theory*, the American critic and practitioner Richard Schechner draws on the work of anthropologist Victor Turner, who sees an essentially dramaturgical, four-step pattern in the development and resolution of social crises: first, a breach of normal social relations; a consequent crisis; redressive action being taken; and, finally, either reintegration of the divided group or the acceptance of the schism.[11]

In his own writing, Turner sees the drama as emphasising the third stage, the ritualised action of redress, where, in anthropological terms, experience is transmitted to other members of a culture for their observation and reflection. Turner defines this space as an area of 'liminality' where normally fixed conditions are open to flux and change, and societies as well as individuals undertake periodic mental reorganisations.[12] It's easy to recognise the liminal space as the realm of nature rather than culture, the magic forest or the blasted heath.

The outdoor liminal space is one of those elements common to both comedy and tragedy which subsequent playwrights continued to explore. As Anne Barton points out in an essay on the dramaturgy of parks, the forest begins to hand over to the park even in Shakespeare: *The Merry Wives of Windsor* ends in Windsor Great Park; editors usually locate *Love's Labour's Lost* in a royal park; and, after winter gives way to spring, even *As You Like It*'s Forest of Arden becomes domesticated.[13] Like the outside locations in *Romeo and Juliet*, the park in *Titus Andronicus* has a comic/Arcadian and a tragic/deathly character: being variously 'green' and 'dreadful'.[14] So it's no surprise that, during the

Restoration, the park takes on many characteristics of the Shakespearian forest, in which a relaxation of traditional social constraints (and the wearing of masks and vizards) allows women in particular to emancipate themselves, much as Shakespeare's cross-dressing heroines are also emancipated. 'The hours of Park-walking are times of perfect Carnival to the Women,' announces Sir Harry Peerabout in the anonymous 1733 play *St James's Park*, an Arcadia in which an evening rendezvous 'was usually regarded as tantamount to sexual surrender'.[15] On top of the masks, there is literal cross-dressing in Farquhar's *The Recruiting Officer*, a play in which one sort of countryside (the world of the camp) invades a country town, the heroine withdraws to the real countryside to change from a woman into a man, and chooses a public walk rather than a house to experiment with her new identity. Sometimes identities are not so much invented as borrowed: in Pierre de Marivaux's *Slave Island*, four characters are washed up on an island whose Prospero-type ruler insists they swap personae (a device borrowed effectively – though possibly unknowingly – by screenwriters Kim Fuller and Jamie Curtis for the Spice Girls movie *Spice World*). And the countryside proper persists as a starting point, a place of refuge and a final destination: John Vanbrugh's *The Relapse* moves from the city to the country and back again; in William Wycherley's *The Country Wife*, the manners and ways of rural life invade the town. At the end of George Etherege's *The Man of Mode*, the rake Dorimant promises to spend a morally recuperative period in Hampshire, just as the king's party pledges to remain in the park of Navarre in *Love's Labour's Lost*. At the end of Molière's *The Misanthrope*, Alceste too decides to flee the vice-ridden city for the wilderness.

The German playwright Heinrich von Kleist made a career out of recasting comedies as tragedies and vice versa: his version of Plautus's double-confusion farce *Amphitryon* is a kind of tragedy; his comedy *The Broken Jug* – in which a judge tries a crime of which he is himself guilty – has the same basic action as *Oedipus*. The comic pseudo-death also continues, up to and beyond Jack Worthing's entrance – in full mourning, down to a black-bordered handkerchief – into the bright summer sunshine of his country garden, in order to announce the death of his invented brother Ernest.

The Importance of Being Earnest contains an impressively comprehensive menu of traditional comedy elements, containing at its core not only a move from the corrupt city to an idyllic countryside (in which more than one person is forced into disguise), but the classic structure of two men facing obstacles to their romantic ambitions. The particular brilliance of Wilde's plotting is to make one of the young lovers the obstacle to the other: Jack's marriage to Gwendolen is opposed by her mother Lady Bracknell, Algie's marriage to Cecily by her guardian Jack; a twist which makes the ending of the play so uniquely neat.

The last two lines of the play hint at the presence of another traditional comic element. Lady Bracknell berates her nephew Jack for 'displaying signs of triviality', to which Jack responds by asserting that, on the contrary, 'I've now realised for the first time in my life the vital Importance of Being Earnest.' The pun on the name by which he has secured the affection of Lady Bracknell's daughter Gwendolen disguises a profounder comic meaning: in becoming Ernest the bridegroom-to-be, Jack has necessarily killed off Ernest the man-about-town. The pretend death in comedy is matched by a metaphorical death. If the reversal in tragedy often consists of the unpredictably devastating consequences of achieving an objective, so the twist in comedy is unexpected loss. It is clear what the comic hero or heroine gains in the liminal zone, less obvious what they have to leave behind. The reversal of comedy is the loss that goes with the gain, the mourning of what is left behind on the island or in the forest. At its most painful in *Henry IV*, most delicate in *As You Like It* and most obvious in *The Tempest* (but also present in plays as various as *The Recruiting Officer*, *She Stoops to Conquer*, *The Misanthrope* and *The Government Inspector*), it is the forfeiture of magic, the disappearance of the power to transform. When the newly crowned King Henry V says to Falstaff, 'I know thee not, old man', he is saying goodbye to the magical part of himself, the part that is disguised, that is irresponsible, that is free. As Henry V, Hal makes one return visit to the magic kingdom – outside, in the camp at Agincourt the night before the battle. But after that he has to return for ever to his newly conquered real one.

Radical and conservative readings

There is a final link between the two traditional genres. I argued that the story of Sophocles' *Oedipus* can be interpreted in two ways: it could mean that, once moral law is violated, you can't defy fate; that we are all as flies to the wanton gods. But as emplotted by Sophocles it actually implies the reverse: that we have free will, that our actions have consequences, which could be avoided if we acted in a different way. All of Shakespeare's great tragic heroes – Richard II, Richard III, Hamlet, Macbeth, Lear, Othello, Antony, Cleopatra, Timon, Coriolanus – die because they make mistakes. They could all have lived and died otherwise.

Comedy has two meanings as well. There is a radical view that comedy is a challenge to the social order, that the disguises and pretences and schemes of the young outflank the hide-bound conservatism of the old. This is the view of comedy as a kind of festive upending of existing, fixed social relations that is described in Mikhail Bakhtin's *Rabelais and His World*:

> All those forms of protocol and ritual based on laughter and consecrated by tradition existed in all the countries of medieval Europe; they were sharply distinct from the serious, official, ecclesiastical, feudal and political cult forms and ceremonials. They offered a completely different, non-official, extra-ecclesiastical and extra-political aspect of the world, of man, and of human relations; they built a second world and a second life outside officialdom, a world in which all medieval people participated more or less, in which they lived during a given time of the year... It belongs on the borderline between art and life. In reality, it is life itself, but shaped according to a certain pattern of play.[16]

But listen to Charles Lamb's reverberant response to Restoration Comedy:

> I could never connect those sports of a witty fancy in any shape with any result to be drawn from them to imitation in real life. They are a world of themselves almost as much as fairy land... I am glad for a season to take an airing beyond the diocese of the strict conscience – not to live always in the precincts of the law courts – but now

and then, for a dreamwhile or so, to imagine a world with
no meddling restrictions... I wear my shackles more
contentedly for having respired the breath of imaginary
freedom.[17]

Certainly, Lamb recognised the anarcho-utopian character of
Arcadia. But there is more than a hint here of what Marxists
used to call repressive tolerance, the festive as a safety valve,
the essential temporality of the allowed fool. The carnival is
pleasurable because it will be over; as will Bottom's dream. In
this view of comedy, the rite of passage is from the indulgences
of childhood to the obligations of adulthood; the action is not
rebellion but incorporation. When the disguises are thrown off,
and the newlyweds return to the city, the gates are closed
behind them.

Both comedy and tragedy, then, can be read conservatively
(human beings are bound to succumb to authority or fate) or
radically (however inadequately, human beings can change
their circumstances). Not surprisingly, when modernism cut
humanity loose from the shackles that had bound art to
convention, it was the resistance of the individual to authority
which would dominate genre in the twentieth century.

Modern genres

Traditional genres now

The twentieth century saw a huge proliferation of genres, many
of which took theatrical form. There continued to be plays you
could call tragedies or comedies, though the change in social,
historical and ideological context meant that they often
referred to and commented on their genre rather than fully
inhabiting it. In *The Death of Tragedy*, George Steiner argued
persuasively that the Marxist belief in an inevitable and benign
resolution to the problem of history demoted high drama from
a lament at the contradictions of the human condition to a
critique of false consciousness.[18] In comedy, you could argue
that changes in nineteenth-century social legislation freed
women from the obligation to marry men their fathers chose
for them, and thus destroyed the social basis of the new comedy

(after nearly 2,500 years) at a stroke of Queen Victoria's pen. In the post-Victorian era, traditional comedy is skewed by Shaw (women refuse to marry anyone at all) and reminted by Noël Coward (the obstacle to marriage no longer being parental, but psychological; the structure of most twentieth-century romantic comedy).

Persistent echoes remained. Brecht's *Galileo* and *Mother Courage and Her Children* are both seen as tragedies of waste, in which the protagonist fails to live up to or understand their place in history. Both Brecht and Beckett see the countryside as a place of confrontation with the fates: it is in the stripped and barren countryside that Mother Courage comes closest to understanding her complicity with the war; it's in a similar landscape that Vladimir instructs Estragon to pull up his trousers at the end of *Waiting for Godot*.

At the same time, plays have continued to search for magic islands and forests into which to banish their characters, whether those islands are weekend country houses, unclimbed alpine peaks, ocean liners, impossible worlds like J.M. Barrie's Neverland in *Peter Pan*, or alternative futures. In *Dear Brutus*, Barrie thrusts the inhabitants of a country-house weekend into a garden, where they experience the lives they could have had, had things been different. In J.M. Synge's *The Well of the Saints*, two blind beggars are given their sight back, and find that the real world they see (including each other) is inferior to the imaginary world they had created, and so return to blind contentment. Indeed, much of Synge's work is set in the future conditional (like Chekhov's). Throughout *The Playboy of the Western World*, the villagers posit alternative explanations of a mysterious young man's arrival in their midst: maybe, speculates the pub owner, he has committed larceny. Or perhaps his land has been grabbed. Or he might be a forger, or have married three wives. Similarly, when the young man announces that he has killed his father, the first response of his listeners is not to ask him how, but to outline the various possibilities (shooting, knifing, hanging) to a degree which renders the man's actual story (inflated though it is) a kind of disappointment. The publican's daughter, Pegeen Mike, weaves elaborate fantasies of a new and better life, even finding time to speculate about the future life her erstwhile fiancé might enjoy with someone else (a 'radiant lady with droves of bullocks on the plains of Meath'). The present-tense plot of *The Playboy* is merely the trunk from which the branches of speculation grow and multiply.

The kind of Arcadian utopia dreamt of by the displaced lords of *As You Like It* and *The Tempest* pops up again in plays in which communal living is tried and fails, like Arnold Wesker's *I'm Talking About Jerusalem* (a rural commune) and Paul Kember's *Not Quite Jerusalem* (a kibbutz). Howard Brenton's *Magnificence* begins in an urban squat and his *Weapons of Happiness* ends in a rural one. In his *Greenland*, the liminal zone is seven hundred years in the future. Echoing Shakespeare's liking for ceremonial confusion, the first act of Brenton and David Hare's black farce *Brassneck* ends with the question: 'My God, if that was the wedding what the hell will they do for the funeral?'

The contemporary genre of the more-than-you-bargained-for-package-holiday play – of which John Godber is the master but Willy Russell's *Shirley Valentine* probably the most notable single example – is an echo of Shakespearian Arcadia. Other examples include Ted Whitehead's *Mecca*, which paints a distinctly unArcadian picture of the British abroad. Louise Page's *Salonika* is set on a Greek holiday beach, but the magic territory its characters enter is the First World War. John Osborne's *The Hotel in Amsterdam* is about the weekend bolt-hole of the employees of a tyrannical film producer, and it's tempting to see the burgeoning genre of plays set in lavatories – Maureen Duffy's *Rites*, Willy Russell's *Stags and Hens*, Stephanie Dale's *Locked*, Rebecca Prichard's *Essex Girls* – as a minor-key refraction of the bolt-hole play. Noël Coward's *Hay Fever* is set during the country-house weekend from hell, and *Private Lives* starts on a honeymoon.

So, there are echoes enough of the vocabulary of the traditional genres, and – particularly – of these comic elements which call the tragic to mind (and vice versa). However, what has mainly happened over the last hundred years is not a reinvention of the ancient genres but the invention of new ones.

Twentieth-century genres

In 1806, the German critic Adam Müller asserted that drama should stand 'between the marketplace and the church... serving as a link between the concerns of everyday life and those of eternity. Tragedy, of course, tends toward religion, comedy towards trade.'[19] This is a good truth in itself, but it contained a peculiar piece of prophecy, because it was, of course, in the succeeding century that theatre divided, as did the other storytelling arts, between the church and the marketplace in a metaphorical sense. You can exaggerate the homogeneity of the theatre audience before 1800 – there was a whole strand of participatory folk art, as distant from the canon we now receive as soap opera is from the repertoire of the National Theatre. But as an audience for simple and popular entertainment entered the marketplace in ever larger numbers in the nineteenth century, the division between the high and the popular grew ever more prominent, until, at the end of the century, a new medium appeared, apparently invented with the sole purpose of providing the exciting and popular bits of dramatic fiction without having to bother at all with its pretensions to profundity. The sensational forms of the ancient genres found their purest means of expression in the cinema. At first, it did so with genres it had borrowed from the theatre (melodrama and farce), then from popular literature (thrillers, science fiction, whodunnits and horror), and, finally, with genres it invented for itself (Westerns and gangster films).

The negotiation between the genres developed in and for the marketplace and those still claiming higher pretensions is the story of twentieth-century drama.

Citing Polonius's infinitely expanding list of dramatic genres in *Hamlet* ('tragedy, comedy, history, pastoral, pastoral-comical, historical-pastoral, tragical-historical, tragical-comical-historical-pastoral...'), John Lennard and Mary Luckhurst demonstrate that the more precise you get in defining genre, the more they proliferate.[20] There seem to me to be three useful ways of defining (and confining) contemporary genre: by their **milieu** (the setting and the people in it), by their **action** (what basic kind of dramatic movement is implied) and by the character of the **protagonist**.

Genre as milieu

Defining genres by milieu gives us the most typical and recognisable set of instances: the Western, the thriller, science fiction, and spy, war, and horror stories. Some – like the Western – are defined primarily by their setting; others – like spy and war stories – by the principal activity being conducted. There is one minor genre – the disaster or location-in-peril movie – in which the setting is the protagonist.

There are two further, extremely durable, popular genres, one implying a very particular and large set of roles, the other essentially a two- or three-hander, both of which glory in imagining ever more distinct and original locations. The classic, golden-age **whodunnit**'s elements include: a defined community of persons suspected of a murder, one of whom will have committed it; a detective of unusual powers, and sometimes an assistant, competitor or superior; an investigation of the crime through interviewing suspects and the exploration of forensic evidence; a second crime (often committed to protect the author of the first); unexplained clues and as-yet-unclear significances, red herrings and false accusations; the assemblage of all suspects; the revelation of the true murderer; and the clearing-up of final points ('There's still one thing I don't understand...'). The number of necessary elements and roles implies an equally formidable table of rules: as early as 1929, Ronald Knox collated Ten Commandments for Detective Fiction, including proscriptions against supernatural agency, Chinamen, more than one secret room or passage, hitherto undiscovered poisons, twins or doubles, and 'unaccountable instinct' or 'exceptional powers of disguise'. Knox also ruled out stories in which the detective committed the crime, which would (of course) remove the longest-running whodunnit (or longest-running anything) from the London stage.

Because of the strict limitations of the form (which, for all the profusion of the genre, remains largely intact) detective fiction seeks ever more imaginative and surprising settings (hence, the tendency for cinema adaptations of Agatha Christie's Poirot novels to transfer stories set in England into exotic foreign locations). This is true of the second, much less rule-bound genre, **romantic comedy**. The detective novelist

P.D. James points out that, although clearly a romantic comedy, Jane Austen's *Emma* is structurally a whodunnit (the puzzle being to identify whom Emma is to marry, from a short but various list of contenders). Certainly, the elegance and ingenuity with which the romcom writer delays the coming together of the couple provides much of the charm of the art. In Nora Ephron's *When Harry Met Sally* it's a pledge; in her *Sleepless in Seattle* it's physical separation; in Peter Howitt's *Sliding Doors* it's an alternative reality.

The major change in the whodunnit is the decline of the private detective. The professionalisation of the sleuth has attached the whodunnit to the precinct drama, a class of genre in which the protagonist is a group (whether assembled in a police station or hospital, or on a spaceship). But, even if constrained within a precinct, the detective can work on his own. Contemporary whodunnits operate on a contested border between the collective, gangshow model of the police procedural, and the world of the isolated, maverick gumshoe, pursuing a lonely, individual course against the opposition of time-serving seniors or up-and-coming whizz-kids, aided only by a loyal if oddly coupled sidekick.

The gumshoe/gangshow dichotomy extends into other forms, genre and media. One of the (many) reasons why the BBC's definition of genre is unhelpful is because it obscures the intriguing relationship between the forms of the serial and the series in their infinite variants, and the genres which that theoretical infinity enables. The main generic peculiarity of **soap opera** appears to be negative: soaps don't end, and so their writers are denied the most generically specific weapon in their armoury. But, actually, for all the openness of their structure and the distinctiveness of their milieus, soaps have considerable generic particularities. We've already noted the common menu of roles, and few soaps operate without two or three particular public locations (the pub, the corner shop, places of work). Alone among dramatic television genres, soaps operate in a kind of real time (their Monday is our Monday, their Christmas is our Christmas). Increasingly, their open-endedness allows for interactive participation by audiences: partly by dramaturgical second-guessing around the water-cooler, increasingly through consultation (either promoted by the companies or bubbling up on fansites from below). This was seen most dramatically in public campaigns to free *The Archers'* Susan Carter, *Coronation Street's* Deirdre Rachid and *Brookside's* Beth Jordache from prison. *The Sun* devoted a double-page spread to the results of a reader survey as to how Grant should be written out of *EastEnders*. And, of course, soaps have multiple protagonists. Outside the police precinct, they are the most obvious example of a gangshow.

By contrast, the **sitcom** – a genre inhabiting the form of the theoretically infinite series – tends to conform to the gumshoe model. True, there are British gangshow sitcoms, like David Croft and Jimmy Perry's *Dad's Army* and *It Ain't Half Hot, Mum*. But the classic British sitcom is built round quirky, dissatisfied central characters, trapped within unsatisfactory situations, facing a theoretically endless series of equivalent predicaments. Often these involve unsuccessful escape attempts, either by young people seeking to escape the old or those in authority (*Steptoe and Son*, *Blackadder*) or the middle-aged/elderly attempting to resolve comparable crises (*One Foot in the Grave*, *Absolutely Fabulous*, *Hancock*, *Till Death Us Do Part*). The fact that the episodes of a great sitcom like *Fawlty Towers* can be seen in any order (who remembers which was the first?) demonstrates their essential circularity. And there is, of course, nothing more circular than intergenerational conflict: great sitcom characters who are threatened by the younger generation veer from Alf Garnett and Albert Steptoe to Edina Monsoon and David Brent.

From the '50s to the '70s, gumshoe drama was a major strain in British stage drama (flawed, isolated, pained but articulate gumshoe protagonists dominate the plays of John Osborne, Simon Gray and David Hare). In the '90s, British drama was suddenly awash with predominantly male gangshows, from gay feel-glad plays like Jonathan Harvey's *Beautiful Thing* and gay feel-sad plays like Kevin Elyot's *My Night with Reg*, via boys' bonding plays like Tim Firth's *Neville's Island* and Patrick Marber's *Dealer's Choice*, to girl-in-a-boys'-gang plays like Rebecca Prichard's *Fair Game* and Mark Ravenhill's *Shopping and Fucking* (not to mention the subgenre of girls-in-and-out-of-a-boys'-bonding play, of which genre Terry Johnson's *Dead Funny* remains the market leader).

Genre actions

A second way of looking at genres is by way of the hooks used by movie and television professionals to describe them. Some of these are no more than vernacular variations or subdivisions of familiar categories: stalk'n'slash, slice'n'dice, and splatter movies all fall under the horror heading; madcap and caper movies are contemporary farces; bodice-rippers are romances set in the past; tearjerkers and sob stories are romances which end sadly. Other hooks imply actions: the buddy movie suggests, and the odd couple demands, that two unlikely people end up working successfully together (as the Titanic Struggle implies that they don't). Other hooks encapsulating dramatic actions include the rite of passage, coming of age and loss of innocence – all of them variants of what nineteenth-century German critics called the *Bildungsroman* or *Entwicklungsroman* (stories of personal formation, the first about the move from childhood to adulthood, the second extending further through life). *Entwicklungsroman* actions also include rags to riches, virtue triumphant and fatal flaw, as well as the comeback kid, the one last stand, dashed hopes and coming to terms. Throwing characters into new and challenging situations creates fish out of water, innocents abroad, new brooms and (sometimes) conspiracies of silence; relationships can consist of spiders and flies, role reversals or eternal triangles; doomed autumnal (or holiday) romances might prove to be dangerous liaisons or their variant fatal attractions; while worms turn, biters are bit and stars are born.

Many of these actions can cross genre boundaries: war movies and Westerns often contain odd couples and consist of rites of passage; stars aren't just born in showbiz movies; eternal triangles initiate whodunnits as well as romances. But the action is a useful way of thinking about genre because it demonstrates that – like comedy and tragedy – one genre is often another genre in masquerade. John Wayne said he'd never do a movie that couldn't be rewritten as a Western; Broadway composer and lyricist David Yazbek points out that Simon Beaufoy's *The Full Monty* is fundamentally a sports story. The assemblage of the team, with its disparate talents but common purpose, is a common component of the sports story, of course, but also a staple of the Western, the war movie, the precinct drama and the fairy tale.

Hooks move us from thinking about genre as a milieu to analysing its meaning. Is there a way of thinking about contemporary genre which deals with both? In his analysis of Hollywood Westerns, *Sixguns and Society*, Will Wright argues that all character and plot functions are derived from four oppositions: good/bad, inside/outside society, strong/weak, and wilderness/civilisation.[21] So, the hero can be strong, good, outside society and from the wilderness, while the villain is bad, strong, inside society and civilised. In another plot, the hero might be inside society or the villain out on the range. The model has been criticised for leaving certain Westerns out, but it also has the problem of focus: is the defining characteristic of a particular Western its hero, its villain, or its landscape? But the good/bad and strong/weak dichotomies are particularly helpful when applied to the central force in the story.

The protagonist model of genre

Applying these dichotomies not just to Westerns but to all kinds of stories boils a multiplicity of genres down to three fundamental structures. Based on the nature of the protagonist, these ur-genres combine and contain many existing genres, but while location is abandoned as a definitional tool, all three consist of (or embrace) recognisable kinds of story, of which audiences have particular and distinct expectations. They are the **adventure** story, the **romance** and the **crime** story.

In the **adventure** story, the protagonist is strong and good. He – as it usually is – has a clear project, to overcome an obstacle and achieve a goal. The adventure story easily inhabits many of the most familiar milieus I listed above. In some adventure stories, the protagonist completes his project without any noticeable reversal ('Despite many obstacles, James Bond or Indiana Jones or Batman defeats the villain and wins the girl'). However, many adventure stories follow the project/reversal pattern I proposed for more complex dramas.

The reversal might be external: 'The Western hero saves the town from the outlaw, but is rejected by the community he has saved'; 'The spy succeeds in his mission, but he is abandoned by HQ in enemy territory.'

The reversal can also be internal: many classic, gung-ho British war movies end with the survivor of an operation (or its initiator) wondering if the gain was worth the sacrifice. The last line of the penultimate scene of *The Longest Day* (adapted by a five-strong screenwriting team from Cornelius Ryan's D-Day novel) is a wounded soldier asking, 'I wonder who won?' Almost all spy stories suggest that – in order to defeat the enemy – the agent has to turn into his opponent. This is a common reversal in the hard-boiled detective story and the film noir; Frank S. Nugent's *The Searchers* is one of many great Westerns in which the pursuer is corrupted by the pursuit.

The value of the good and strong protagonist having some kind of flaw accounts, perhaps, for the kind of environments in which adventure stories flourish, both in single and multiple-episode form. Doctors and policemen are presumed to be inherently trustworthy, and it is dramatically powerful to discover they have feet of clay (this may explain repeated failures to create precinct dramas set in the worlds of journalism, or – until *The West Wing* – politics). The basic characteristics of the fictional detective – ordinary-looking, a bit of an outsider, with a good memory, a ready wit, a taste for drink and an unexpected hobby – were established in the first complete British whodunnit, Wilkie Collins' 1868 *The Moonstone*, which has remained the template ever since.

In the **romance**, the protagonist is good and (in the sense of physical or institutional power) weak. Like the adventure story, the action of a romance can conform to the simple 'despite... nonetheless' model. However, the romantic project is not immune to irony. In classical romance, the reversal applies not to the happy couple, but to those other characters (including, in the case of *The Merchant of Venice*, an outwitted father) who are left out of the general rejoicing, thereby reminding us that the happiest of love-matches may go sour. A frequent twentieth-century romantic reversal is provided by the warring couple for whom the only thing worse than living together is living apart; in Nora Ephron's *When Harry Met Sally* (and Noël Coward's *Private Lives*, for that matter), the protagonists' joint project is to keep apart, and the twist their failure to do so. Throughout history, women in fictional romances have sought to win men who have not wanted to be won; 'taming' *of* a woman provides the title of Shakespeare's least attractive comedy, but much, much more frequently, the tamer is the woman, from Jane Eyre to Bridget Jones. In *All's Well That Ends Well*, Helen sets out to tame Bertram; in *Much Ado About Nothing*, the taming of Benedick and Beatrice is undertaken by their friends.

In *Romeo and Juliet*, the catastrophe is brought about by the resilience of the obstacle; the couple set out to tame the feud, but fail. In twentieth-century romantic tragedy, too, the reversal is provided by the strength of circumstance: in the case of Noël Coward's *Still Life* (filmed as *Brief Encounter*), social convention; in Julius J. Epstein, Philip G. Epstein and Howard Koch's *Casablanca*, an overriding obligation. In the subgenre of doomed-affair movies (including Jo Heims and Dean Riesner's *Play Misty for Me* and James Dearden and Nicholas Meyer's *Fatal Attraction*), the reversal is provided by the loved person turning out to be other than what they seem.

It's entertaining to speculate whether there is or could be an effective story with a weak and bad protagonist. There are many in which the protagonist is bad and strong. The **crime** genre embraces Aeschylus's *Agamemnon*, Shakespeare's *Macbeth* and *Richard III*, and many of the best movies ever made.

Because most of them end badly (for the protagonist), many crime stories operate in tandem with other genres. In most whodunnits, the crime story of the murder is followed by the adventure story of its investigation; contemporary thrillers habitually tell the story of the crime in parallel with the pursuit of its perpetrator (so Frederick Forsyth's *The Day of the Jackal* has two protagonists: the assassin planning to murder Charles de Gaulle and the policeman striving to stop him). Screenwriter Stephen de Souza insists that, in textbook terms, the protagonists of the *Die Hard* movies are the villains: it is their aim and obstacles we follow.

The other particularity of the crime story is the balance between the project and the reversal. The reversal of many adventure stories and romances is acknowledged only in the closing moments (classically, Ethan Edwards' lonely march into the wilderness at the end of *The Searchers*, and Rick Blaine's airfield parting from Ilsa Lund in the closing moments of *Casablanca*). However effective the criminal's project, the point of a crime story lies in its reversal. If the adventure hero is often a good man with a flaw, then the crime protagonist's redeeming feature (if he has one) is his understanding of the ultimate futility of his endeavour. Jerry Palmer makes this point, drawing on Robert Warshow's telling comparison between the gangster and the Western hero:

> The gangster story is typically a story of successful enterprise followed by dramatic failure; although the enterprise is criminal, even evil, the final failure is presented not as punishment but as defeat... His failure is a central part of his attraction, for it shows that the will to succeed is nugatory.[22]

For the Westerner, what's really at stake is not material goods nor even power, but his honour. So, while it doesn't matter whether the Westerner wins or loses, 'the gangster's final defeat entails the admission that his whole life has been a mistake'.[23] The crime-story protagonist realises that however powerful he may have become, he will never be safe or secure; for all he has gained he has lost the one thing that matters. There is no 'despite... nonetheless' action in crime stories.

Finally, all three ur-genres can operate in the realms of the unearthly. While the milieu of the science-fiction adventure is radically different from that of other adventure stories, the basic action is often indistinguishable from more naturalistic adventure stories (science fiction is certainly a genre to which you could apply the John Wayne test, set as it often is in 'space, the final frontier'). Superman's powers are merely a bodily ingestion of the magic weapons or abilities which are granted by donors to the heroes of folktales. Like the crew of the Starship Enterprise, Odysseus boldly went where nobody had gone before.

The point of the superhero's powers is that, although they may come and go, they are consistent, logical and known. In the supernatural variant of the romance genre – the ghost story – the supernatural force is arbitrary, mysterious and protean. Once again, the romantic protagonist pits her moral authority against forces much stronger and more powerful than herself.

Were Lucy to be the protagonist of Bram Stoker's *Dracula* (which she isn't), then you could see it as a romance of this type. In fact, *Dracula* is an example of the supernatural form of the crime story. There are three great nineteenth-century horror actions whose protagonists shun human society in order to play God, but who discover that the only thing worse than the limitations of human existence is to be freed of them. In Robert Louis Stevenson's *Dr Jekyll and Mr Hyde*, a man seeks to evade responsibility for his crimes by dividing himself into two. Mary Shelley's Frankenstein assumes God's role as the creator. Dracula aspires to live for ever. All three succeed for a while, but the Promethean presumption of their project brings about their downfall. Man's doomed attempt to surmount the limitations of his earthly life is a reading of tragedy appropriate to our times. *Dr Jekyll and Mr Hyde*, *Frankenstein* and *Dracula* are not the greatest novels ever written, but they are among the greatest stories ever told.

Why bother with genre?

This is a long chapter, and that points up a paradox. In looking at contemporary, post-1900 genres, I've had to draw my examples largely from the novel, television and film. There is a reason for this. As early as 1960, Peter Brook noticed that genre enables the fickle television viewer to tell immediately who's the hero and who's the villain, and 'to guess at the part of the story he's missed'.[24] Now, in the age of multiple-channel-surfing, the recognisable landmarks provided by genre are even more vital, in order to keep track of where you are.

However, you can't channel-hop in theatre. Unless you're late, or you fall asleep, you have no choice but to follow the whole story. Theatre doesn't need to appeal to the mass, popular audience which is (supposedly) attracted by the familiarity of genre expectation. None of the new genres of the twentieth century began in theatre. You could say that one of contemporary theatre's great virtues – almost, its *raison d'être*

– is that it isn't imprisoned within the confines of genre storytelling. How splendid it is not to identify the hero and the villain in the first five minutes. What a relief to spend an entire evening discovering that there isn't really a villain or a hero there at all.

So, if not being trapped in genre is one of the great glories of modern theatre, why spend so much time talking about it? There are four main reasons. The first is that, as I've argued, the patterns and meanings of traditional genre have come down to us, sometimes fully fledged as contemporary comedy or tragedy, more often as references, borrowings and echoes.

The second reason is that, although theatre didn't invent any of the new popular genres of the twentieth century, it has borrowed many, both straight-up and in cannibalised or satirised form. Though stage Westerns seem confined to musicals (with the notable exception of Snoo Wilson's *The Glad Hand*), there are stage whodunnits and thrillers, spy, ghost and horror stories, and war plays. Charles Wood's *Dingo* and *Jingo* are both war plays; Peter Nichols, John McGrath and Arnold Wesker have written plays based on their experience of national service. Jez Butterworth's *Mojo* draws on the argot of the British gangster movie; Bryony Lavery's *Her Aching Heart* is a spoof bodice-ripper. Tom Stoppard satirised whodunnits in *The Real Inspector Hound*, and David Hare the hard-boiled detective genre in *Knuckle*.

Third, if theatre hasn't developed contemporary genres with as comprehensive a menu of elements as the Western or the whodunnit, it has certainly come up with what you could call 'soft genres', stories which share perhaps a subject, maybe a way of telling, a milieu or an action, common elements which although individually elusive may reach a sufficiently critical mass to tempt audiences to compare them to other plays which draw from the same menu. In the mid-twentieth century, theatre exploited its intensity and its architecture in courtroom dramas. In the 1960s, David Storey made a career out of plays set during the preparation and undertaking of a piece of a work, in *The Contractor* (the erection and dismantling of a wedding marquee), *The Changing Room* (before, during and after a rugby-league match) and *Life Class* (as its name implies), a soft genre to which Arnold Wesker had already contributed with

The Kitchen and to which Stephen Jeffreys was later to add with *A Going Concern*. Many of the female playwrights who emerged in the 1980s wrote about what they saw as the invisible relationship of mother and daughter, in plays which suggested that each new generation of women strives not to repeat the mistakes of the preceding one. In the 1990s, the AIDS epidemic provided an obvious basis for gay tragedy; it was also possible to detect a simple action in many gay comedies (Act 1: son comes out, Act 2: Mum comes to terms). Many Afro-Caribbean plays follow the pattern of a young man trying to break out of a criminal subculture, often through love, and failing. Many plays by young Asian women are about families in which the father pursues doomed projects, the daughter is dating out of the faith, the son is involved in drugs or thinking of going off to join the fighters, and the mother is trying to hold the family together. In all these cases, critics complained that the gay play or the black play or the Muslim play had grown tiresomely homogenous. In all these cases, audiences came because the plays were addressing concerns that mattered, deeply and properly, and not just to them.

Finally, there's a subject whose treatment may not be common enough to warrant being called a genre, but which certainly implies a structural form. Sebastian Barry writes plays in which the dying bring back their past and present ghosts at the moment of death. Tom Stoppard's *The Invention of Love* is about an old man reconstructing the story of his life, not entirely reliably (one of the best scenes is a conversation between an older and younger version of the same man). Michael Frayn's *Copenhagen* consists of the ghosts of two nuclear scientists and one of their wives, reconstructing a number of possible versions of one actual fifteen-minute conversation between the scientists in occupied Denmark during the war. They are among literally dozens of plays written in the 1990s and the 2000s which explore the credibility and usages of memory.

Echoes of traditional genres, borrowings of modern ones, the detection of generic correspondence between similar kinds of contemporary play: taken together, there is enough genre in the contemporary theatre to encourage audiences to look out for particular outcomes, and for playwrights to need to bear that in mind. At the very least, it provides playwrights with opportunities to deny or subvert those expectations.

It also invites audiences to apply techniques which it has developed for reading different genres to the reading of different dramatic structures. If twentieth-century theatre has merely borrowed genres developed in the novel and cinema, it has been remarkably formally inventive. Historically, different structures have lent themselves to different genres (from the real-time Greek tragedy to three-act plays in which the liminal zone is Act 2). Now, it is as hard to challenge audiences' presumptions about the meaning of plays which have unconnected plots, run backwards, or go back to the beginning at the end, as it is to deny their expectations of different sorts of story.

1. Jonathan Culler, *Literary Theory*, Oxford: Oxford University Press, 1997, p. 73.

2. John Lennard and Mary Luckhurst, *The Drama Handbook: A Guide to Reading Plays*, Oxford: Oxford University Press, 2002, p. 52.

3. Terence Hawkes, *Structuralism and Semiotics*, London: Methuen, reprinted by Routledge, London, 1989, p. 104.

4. Quoted in Marvin Carlson, *Theories of the Theatre*, Ithaca, New York: Cornell University Press, 1984, p. 26.

5. *Ibid.* p. 22.

6. *Ibid.* p. 137.

7. Eric Bentley, *The Life of the Drama*, London: Methuen, 1965, p. 261.

8. Hesketh Pearson, *The Life of Oscar Wilde*, London and New York: Penguin, 1960, p. 202.

9. Northrop Frye, *Anatomy of Criticism*, London and New York: Penguin, 1990, p. 215.

10. J.L. Styan, *The Elements of Drama*, Cambridge: Cambridge University Press, 1963, pp. 52, 56.

11. Richard Schechner, *Essays on Performance Theory*, New York: Drama Book Specialists, 1977, pp. 60-1.

12. Marvin Carlson, *op. cit.*, pp. 508-9.

13. Anne Barton, 'Parks and Ardens', in *Essays, Mainly Shakespearian*, Cambridge: Cambridge University Press, 1994, pp. 354-7, 365.

14. *Ibid.* p. 359.

15. *Ibid.* pp. 368, 370.

16. Mikhail Bakhtin, *Rabelais and His World*, trans. Hélène Iswolsky, Bloomington: Indiana University Press, 1984, pp. 5-7

17. Quoted in Eric Bentley, *op. cit.*, London: Methuen, 1965, pp. 239, 256.

18. George Steiner, *The Death of Tragedy*, London: Faber and Faber, 1961.

19. Marvin Carlson, *op. cit.*, pp. 188-9.

20. John Lennard and Mary Luckhurst, *op. cit.*, p. 50.

21. Will Wright, *Sixguns and Society*, Berkeley and Los Angeles: University of California Press, 1975, p. 49.

22. Jerry Palmer, *Potboilers*, London: Routledge, 1991, p. 92.

23. *Ibid.* p. 93.

24. Peter Brook, *The Shifting Point*, London: Methuen, 1987, p. 26.

5
Structure

Structure

Plays have actions, revealed through the plotting of stories. Those actions and plots may conform to the expectations aroused by different genres. A play doesn't have to function within a genre, and that is one of the virtues of the theatre. But, in all plays, the plot is expressed through a structure, in which the narrative is organised into segments of space and time. Like emplotment, structure is not just a convenient way of organising material, but is a conveyor of meaning.

Anyone who's listened to the playwright Stephen Jeffreys talking about play structure is bound to be indebted to his perceptions, particularly his insight that the time and space divisions which delineate structure are of two types: open and closed. The resultant grid is a hugely effective way of calibrating the playwright's structural options, and it would be perverse to ignore it in this chapter. I give some of the options different titles, and provide different categories when I talk about what Jeffreys calls 'dislocated structures' at the end.

Jeffreys provides two further major insights. One is that every structural form has advantages and disadvantages, from the 'buttered crumpets' problem of real-time plays to the disjuncture of the epic. The other is the rule that, broadly speaking, the smaller the number of scenes, the hotter and more intense the audience's experience.

Structural options

Play structures fall into two categories: those using linear time and those which disrupt it. Using linear time does not mean, of course, that the plot presents the play's narrative in story order;

as we've seen, Sophocles emplotted *Oedipus* so he could tell a story that covered many years, in non-chronological order, in an hour and a half. But *Oedipus*'s stage action is linear: there are no flashbacks, and no segments are presented outside the order in which Sophocles invites us to believe they could have happened, outside the gates of the palace of Thebes.

Oedipus is an example of the first structural category, **real-time**: plays which operate in a single time and place, as a single scene. There are plays which operate in a single time but move from place to place, with only the necessary movement of characters from A to B interrupting the continuous flow, like *The Tempest*, Ibsen's *John Gabriel Borkman*, and Trevor Griffiths's *Comedians*, in which a group of trainee comics rehearse in a college classroom in the first act, perform to a visiting agent in the second act in another location, and return to the college for Act 3.

The second category, that of plays which operate in a **single time cycle in one place**, exploits the neoclassical loophole in Aristotle's unity of time and place rule, by expanding the play's duration beyond real time to a longer but defined (and confined) period, like an evening, a single day or perhaps a weekend. This is the model of most French neoclassical comedies and tragedies; it's also the pattern of Pierre Corneille's warrior romance *Le Cid*, which crams a battle, two duels and a love-match into a twenty-four-hour period, provoking satirists to subtitle the play 'Rodrigue's busy day'. Expanding time also provides the possibility of changing setting, but again, within the confines of a single milieu (a house, an estate, perhaps a town). Examples of single-location, expanded-time plays include Shaw's *Candida* (set in the sitting room of a parsonage at three points in the same day), Noël Coward's *Hay Fever* (set in the hall of a country house over a single weekend), and the numerous Ibsen plays which take place in the same room over a couple of days (including *A Doll's House*, *Ghosts* and *Hedda Gabler*). Other Ibsen plays move around between rooms, and sometimes outside them, within the same time cycle (like *The Wild Duck*, *The Lady from the Sea* and *The Master Builder*), as does Shaw's *Heartbreak House*. Like *The Comedy of Errors*, most Restoration plays – including Etherege's *The Man of Mode* and Farquhar's *The Recruiting Officer* – take place during a single day and night in various parts of a single city or town, a pattern shared with Sheridan's *The Rivals* and Oliver Goldsmith's *She Stoops to Conquer*.

Plays which operate in **stretched time in a limited space** allow sufficiently long time gaps between the scenes or acts for the changes in the characters' circumstances to communicate significant meaning. This is the structural form of Chekhov's *The Seagull* and *Three Sisters*, as well as some of Shaw (including *Arms and the Man* and *Pygmalion*). Noël Coward does it twice: both *Peace in Our Time* and *This Happy Breed* raid particular and confined milieus (a pub and a household) at significant moments in their history, over periods of, respectively, five and thirty-seven years.

Many plays which take their characters from the inside world to the outside world and back again operate in a **stretched time cycle with a changed space**. This is true of Shakespeare's Arcadian comedies, but also of *The Importance of Being Earnest*, Barrie's *Dear Brutus* (where the outside world is an alternative reality), and many of Feydeau's farces (in which, as in Restoration Comedy, the alternative world is a site for illicit sexual liaison). Shaw's *Major Barbara* shuffles its characters from the private to the public world, from a drawing room to a Salvation Army shelter, back to the drawing room and then to an arms factory, over a period of three days.

By contrast, **stretched time in an unlimited space** can take the audience anywhere. Plays of this type include Shakespeare's histories and some of the tragedies (not *Othello*, whose timescale, though notoriously tricky to nail down, certainly covers no more than a week).

Finally, cinema's appropriation of the flashback from the novel gave twentieth-century theatre a whole new structural repertoire. Non-linear structural forms embrace plays with **disrupted time**, in which incidents from the story are put in a different order from their literal chronology (including plays which flash backwards or forwards, or go into reverse); plays with a **double timescale**, in which two stories from different periods are told in parallel (often with the later story investigating, interrogating or remembering the earlier story); and **disconnected time** plays, in which there are several discrete storylines with no immediately apparent connection between them. Late-twentieth-century plays which employ these strategies include Harold Pinter's *Betrayal* and Caryl Churchill's *Top Girls* (disrupted time), Tom Stoppard's *Arcadia* (double time) and Rebecca Prichard's *Essex Girls* (disconnected time).

Each of these structures offers the playwright opportunities; each has significant drawbacks. All have the potential to convey different meanings to the audience.

Linear structures

Real time

The huge virtue of plays set in real time is the intensity of the experience they provide. Real time is our time. It isn't disrupted by scene changes (which draw attention to the artifice of the endeavour); our experience of the events we see portrayed is exactly parallel to its portrayal. Although writing real-time plays is extremely difficult (for reasons outlined below), the form puts up few barriers of artifice to remind the audience of the playwright's presence, removing many of the devices (notably, changes of time and location), which draw attention to the playwright's activity. Real time draws the audience in, and never lets it go.

One difficulty of real time is that you can't avoid the naturalistic inconveniences of real life. When the new director of the festival theatre at Stratford, Ontario, proudly told Laurence Olivier that the arena form of the stage meant you couldn't conceal a thing, Olivier responded: 'Then we're all fucked.' The real-time playwright, too, has nowhere to hide. Real time means that, if a character needs to toast crumpets (or cook a three-course meal) it will take as long as it does in real life, with the penalty that theatre time always seems slower (which accounts for the power of even quite short silences). As if on a well-run campsite, the real-time playwright has to bring everything he or she needs, and take it all away again at the end of the stay. The most mundane processes have to take place before your very eyes: if characters need to enter the building, they either have to possess keys or be admitted by onstage characters (sadly, the butler and the French window are no longer viable options, though the socialist playwright Andy de la Tour managed to find an excuse for the latter – with some chutzpah – in a play about New Labour called *Landslide*).

Real time also presents expositional problems. The intensity of the two-handed conversation (in which there is no third party to mediate, interrogate, or change the subject) often tempts real-time playwrights: however, if our characters know each other, we have to find ways to prevent them spending the early minutes telling each other things they already know, or would be unlikely to have withheld in the past. The latter problem is addressed by the reunion play, which brings two characters back together after a period of time (the model of David Harrower's *Blackbird*, in which a young woman confronts a man with whom she had an affair in her early teens). Real-time plays which seek to combine the advantages of multiple characters with the intensity of two-handed conversations can slip into a kind of interview format, in which one character meets and greets a series of visitors. This can work well if there are enough differences between the tone, character, duration and content of the duologues to obscure their structural similarity, as there are in Trevor Griffiths's *Occupations* (which covers several days) and Christopher Shinn's *Now or Later* (set in real time). Both are set in hotel rooms, one in 1920s Turin during a workers' uprising, and the other in present-day America on election night.

Some of the logistical problems of real time disappear when you have an interval. Although David Hare's *Skylight* feels as if it's in real time, there are three time jumps: one when a character takes a bath; a second when two of them make love and sleep (during the interval); and a third between the end of the main action at around 3 a.m. and an epilogue at dawn. Gaps like this can retain the intensity of real time, while evading buttered crumpets aplenty. The single location suggests that nothing is being hidden away, and it's easy for playwrights to give the impression – should they want to – that little of importance happened between the scenes they have chosen to show.

Ibsen is the master of this technique, and he pays minute attention to the tiny changes that become unmistakably visible and resonant on a single set. In *A Doll's House*, a Christmas tree appears in the first interval ('stripped and dishevelled, with the stumps of burnt-out candles'). In *Ghosts*, the first and second acts are in daylight; in the third it's night, all the doors are open, and we can see the glow of the burning orphanage in the background. At the beginning of Act 2 of *Hedda Gabler* a piano has been moved and a writing desk put in its place; at the beginning of Act 3, in the early morning, curtains are closed and the stove door is open, revealing the dying embers of a fire. Because we're in the same room, and so much else is the same, our attention is drawn to the fact and the import of these tiny changes.

Stretching time and place

Changing locations within or around a house or even a town reduces the impact of small changes in a single set, but opens up much greater opportunities for the setting to communicate meaning. Again, Ibsen strives to make his decisions appear inevitable, to give the impression that the next thing you see and the next place you go are the play's only possible trajectories. So, for example, the second act of *The Wild Duck* overlaps with the first: Hjalmar Ekdal leaves a swanky lunch at the house of a wealthy merchant well before the end of Act 1, appearing at his own meagre apartment a few minutes into Act 2. In *Uncle Vanya* the setting gradually narrows from an afternoon garden, via a dining room at night and a daytime drawing room, to a cluttered office-cum-bedroom in the evening. Shaw's *Heartbreak House*, by contrast, moves outwards, from two acts indoors to a third in the garden (though locations change, the stage action of Acts 2 and 3 are continuous).

The greater the jumps in time and space, the more the audience is invited to consider the alternative plotting possibilities (the play could carry on as was, jump to another day, or go somewhere else), and, thus, to notice and draw meaning from the playwright's choices. Chekhov's *Three Sisters* tells its story through its four settings: the rooms in which we meet the increasingly beleaguered sisters diminish in size, and they end up expelled from the house altogether. But its meaning is also revealed by what's happened to the characters in the eighteen-month gaps between the acts. For Olga, Masha and Irina, their sister-in-law Natasha's growing hold over the household – and her expanding family – is underlined by an increasingly ominous series of public events: the first act is set during a happy saint's day celebration, the second against the background of a town carnival which is banned from the house, the third as a fire rages through the town, and the fourth as the regiment that has brought life to the town, and love to Masha, prepares to march away. Between the acts, the economic, professional and personal fortunes of the sisters have declined. For some characters, however – notably Natasha, but also the old family nurse Anfisa – things have improved. After being spurned by Natasha in the third act, Anfisa now has her own room and her own bed, and has never been happier.

Arthur Miller's play about the seventeenth-century Salem witch-hunt, *The Crucible*, is structured in the same way. The play is in four acts, set in increasingly threatening environments (from bedroom to living room to courtroom to prison) within the same town. The acts are divided by time jumps in which important events occur (as in *Three Sisters* and *The Seagull*): between Acts 1 and 2 a number of women are arrested for witchcraft; between Act 2 and Act 3 the main character John Proctor is arrested and arraigned; and between Acts 3 and 4 there have been rebellions against similar witch-hunts in nearby towns, and Proctor's main accuser has disappeared. Most of the characters have identifiable arcs during the course of the drama, and many of these changes occur during the act breaks.

A variant of the steady progression from scene to different scene in plays like *Three Sisters* and *The Crucible* is the play that is deliberately broken-backed, taking its characters into radically different environments and leaving them there. The first three acts of *Julius Caesar* consist of a stately progression through the conspiracy to the assassination of Caesar and the backlash that follows it; the fourth act introduces a parade of new characters, to populate a battlefield. Similarly, *Timon of Athens* spends its first half in the court and its second, with few of the same characters, on a blasted heath. Many contemporary plays are games of two halves, with two acts unusually similar to each other – as in Beckett's *Waiting for Godot* – or even the same – as in the same writer's *Play*. Alternatively, playwrights

make their two halves startlingly dissimilar: in Caryl Churchill's
Cloud Nine, the same group of characters populate a colonial
outpost in Act 1 and present-day London in Act 2; in Brecht's
The Caucasian Chalk Circle, the first act is about one character,
and the second about another, with the two plots converging at
the very end.

Moving some or all of the characters into a dramatically
different environment and then moving them back again is the
structural strategy most closely connected to a particular genre.
From *A Midsummer Night's Dream* (court – magic forest –
court) via *The Importance of Being Earnest* (townhouse –
country garden – country house) to Barrie's *Dear Brutus*
(country house – magic garden – country house), Arcadian
comedy moves its characters through the compression
chamber of a liminal zone – whether that zone be magical,
fantastical or exotic – and out the other side. Sometimes the
timeframe is confined to a day or two (or even less), sometimes
the characters spend months in the liminal zone (as in *As You
Like It*), sometimes – as in *The Winter's Tale* – the segments are
divided by many years. The power of the form is the way in
which what happens in Act 2 informs and changes the Act 1
environment when we return to it at the end.

Epic theatre

As we've seen, the plays of Ibsen's mature period strive above all
else for a dramatic seamlessness which allows the creation of a
highly concentrated emotional intensity, deceiving the
audience into thinking that the action they are witnessing is
inevitable, and there is no authorial decision-making going on
at all. Brecht's dramatic technique is precisely the reverse. As he
put it in 'A Short Organum for the Theatre', the audience
shouldn't 'fling itself into the story as if it was a river and let
itself be carried vaguely hither and thither'; the individual
scenes of a play must 'be knotted together in such a way that the
knots are easily noticed', so that the audience can interpose its
judgement.[1] While Ibsen strives to make the scenes seem part
of the same gathering movement, the Brecht scene strives to
be as distinct as possible from those which follow and precede

it, to operate like a little play in and of itself. Far from thinking that Scene 3 is the inevitable consequence of Scene 2, Brecht wants us to ask why he's moved us from Venice to Florence, or from a Swedish roadside to a Polish encampment.

The advantage of Brecht's epic theatre lies in its very present-tenseness: there is little need for exposition, we see everything we need to know. The disadvantage is not just that plays with lots of little scenes are harder to engage with, as each new scene requires a new environment to get used to, and often (in Brecht's case) a new group of people to meet; it's also that, by making his choices so visible, the playwright elbows himself in between us and the action, preventing us from identifying wholeheartedly with what's going on. Of course, that's exactly what Brecht wanted to do.

Rightly or wrongly, standing like a border guard between the audience and the action is no longer a fashionable playwriterly approach. How strange, therefore, that the most interesting developments in structure of the last hundred years have sought to make the playwright even more visible.

Non-linear structures

Disrupted time

If the epic theatre empowers the author, then non-linear time disempowers the characters. At least Mother Courage knows what happened to her in the play so far. The whole thrust of a play like Harold Pinter's *Betrayal* – which starts at the end of an adulterous love affair and moves back to its beginning – is that we know more and more about what's going to happen in the characters' lives as the characters know less and less.

The use of disrupted time to demonstrate meaning is most developed in cinema. Harold Ramis and Danny Rubin's 1993 *Groundhog Day* pioneered the broken-record structure, Quentin Tarantino and Roger Avary's 1994 *Pulp Fiction* the loop, Milcho Manchevski's 1994 *Before the Rain* a circular formation, and Jonathan and Christopher Nolan's 2000 *Memento* the switchback. As Roger Luckhurst argues, the 'trauma flashback' that has become such a feature of contemporary cinema dramatised post-traumatic stress and multiple-personality disorder before these conditions were accepted medically (an acceptance to which, Luckhurst suggests, dramatisation contributed). From cinema features like Morton S. Fine and David Friedkin's 1965 *The Pawnbroker* to Stewart Stern's 1976 made-for-TV *Sybil*, the involuntary flashback has been used to dramatise the syndrome by which sufferers from post-traumatic stress disorder fail to store traumatic memories securely in the past, and experience them as if they were happening now.[2]

This use of disrupted time not just for expositional or ironical purposes but to dramatise how memory brings the past to life in the present is the core feature of one of the greatest plays of the last hundred years. Arthur Miller's original title for *Death of a Salesman* was *The Inside of His Head*, and its action is the unravelling of the dreams that the failed salesman Willy Loman had for himself and his sons. The contrast between Loman's dreams and present-day reality is exposed not through reminiscence or the arrival of a character from the past, but by seeing Loman's memories enacted at the moment when they come into his mind. They are not so much flashbacks as projections of the past in the present – certainly they are not flashbacks in the sense that they result from an authorial decision to put the events in a non-linear order (as in Adolph Green and Betty Comden's *Singin' in the Rain*, Joseph L. Mankiewicz's *All About Eve* and countless other mainstream movies). They are, however, akin to the flashbacks in *Citizen Kane*, in which the scenes in the past are mediated through the memory of the investigating journalist's five interlocutors. What is original about *Salesman* is that Loman's memory is unreliable, and that we are invited to witness how these unreliable memories provoke his present actions. The most dramatic example of this technique is Willy's memory of what is clearly a highly mythologised version of his brother Ben, whom Willy recalls entering the African jungle a pauper and coming out the owner of a diamond mine, and who becomes a confidant for Willy as he decides to kill himself, so that his favourite son Biff can build a business career (or rather, Willy's dream of Biff's career) with the life-insurance money.

Memorable and innovatory though this device is, it

occupies no more than a fifth of the stage time. In fact, it was lucky to survive the production process: director Elia Kazan persuaded Miller to group all the 'flashbacks' together as a kind of interlude, only to be overruled by producer Kermit Bloomgarden, whose insistence that 'this piece of shit I will not do' saved a masterpiece.[3] Outside the recollective sections, the play is a present-tense picture of a man who has lived his life based on an illusion and who sees it unravel in a day. That description would fit almost all of Ibsen's mature plays; the difference is that instead of reporting the illusions of the past, Miller has taken a cinematic device and reminted it to demonstrate how it is not the past but our memory of it that informs our actions in the here-and-now.

By making his 'flashbacks' a dramatisation of a character's present thought processes, Miller made his mechanism as authorially invisible as it's possible for a non-naturalistic device to be. Twelve years before *Death of a Salesman* was produced, J.B. Priestley had written a disrupted-time play whose strategy was almost exactly the reverse. In his first play, the 1932 *Dangerous Corner*, Priestley had shown his (sleight of) hand off to the audience, ending a play full of poisonous revelation by going back to the beginning and suggesting that, had the volume of a gramophone been slightly louder, none of the subsequent events and disclosures would have occurred. In his 1937 *Time and the Conways*, Priestley's authorial strategy was even more evident to the audience.

The first act of the play takes place at the twenty-first birthday party of Kay, the eldest daughter of the Conway family, in 1919. As the celebration unfolds, the family looks forward to a glowing future. In Act 2 we jump forward to 1937, to discover that all of the Conways' dreams have been shattered by broken marriages, collapsed careers, failed ideals, financial disasters and a premature death. The third act returns to the 1919 party – literally, a second or two after we left it – to see the disastrous decisions being taken: the marriage proposal is made, the house is put on the market, the inevitability of socialism is ringingly declared.

It's possible to read the play as a flash-forward by one of the characters (Kay is onstage throughout the second act). But, for the audience, the experience is that of learning things the first act characters don't know. For the Conway family, the future is the liminal zone in which they will move from youthful idealism to jaded realism. In that model, Priestley was following Noël Coward's surprisingly innovative, rarely performed 1930 play *Post-Mortem*, which largely consists of a dying First World War soldier's flash-forward vision of a post-war life in which his sacrifice was betrayed. Anticipating Terry Johnson's Freud play *Hysteria*, most of the play takes place in the last seconds of the central character's life, during which Coward's protagonist brings back what he's learnt in the future to report on as he dies. By contrast, when the Conways return to 1919, it's as if they'd never been away. Like *Betrayal*, *Time and the Conways* holds our privileged information about the characters against them.

As, in a different way, do three late-twentieth-century British plays in which the manipulation of stage chronology expresses the plays' action. In all three, the last scene of the plot is taken from the beginning of the story.

David Hare's *Plenty* is about a woman who fought with the Special Operations Executive in France during the Second World War, and whose life gradually falls apart between the end of the war and 1962. The action is: 'A woman spends her youth fighting for a new world, but when it arrives, she finds that it doesn't live up to her expectations.' Hence, the plot decision to put her idealistic expectations of the post-war world – what would be the second scene of the play if you ran it chronologically – at the very end. Set in liberated France in 1944, both the scene and the play ends with the line 'There will be days and days and days like this', at a point when we know perfectly well that there won't be.

Originally read as a debate between feminism and socialism, the enduring action of Caryl Churchill's *Top Girls* is: 'A woman achieves success in business but at the price of an aspect of her womanhood.' The reversal is dramatised by the last scene of the play, in which we discover that the woman has given up her child to be brought up by her sister. But in fact the last scene of the play is the first thing that happens chronologically: it explains much, but in retrospect. Had it been the first scene of the play I think the action would have been reversed, becoming: 'Despite having to make a hard choice, a woman nonetheless succeeds in a man's world.' Reversing the chronology of the play reverses its meaning.

The third play, Charlotte Keatley's *My Mother Said I Never Should*, is a play about four generations of women striving not to repeat the mistakes of their mothers. The play shuffles its three narratives, moving backwards and forwards in time, dramatising the cyclical nature of the women's dreams, demonstrating how they are so frequently dashed, but also showing how later generations can do things earlier generations can't. The play ends with the moment in 1920 when the oldest of the women realises she's in love for the first time, ending with the double-edged statement: 'Really and truly, this is the beginning of my life.'

It's no coincidence that two of these three examples are from plays by women. The major event in new theatre-writing in the Britain of the 1980s was the emergence of a generation of young female playwrights, who sought to express meaning through the manipulation of chronology. In the same way that Brecht invites us to ask why the action in *Galileo* has moved to a ballroom, a marketplace or the Hall of the Collegium in Rome, so Charlotte Keatley's meaning in *My Mother Said I Never Should* is contained in the juxtaposition of scenes not only separated but reshuffled in time (so, not 'Why are we in Florence now?' but 'Why are we in 1951?'). There's an argument that disrupted time is a way of dramatising women's traditional experience, which has often been characterised as more circular and less linear than men's. Some female critics argue that women's way of assembling and learning from that experience is more about making connections between superficially disparate elements than identifying straightforward progressions of cause and effect. Whatever the strength of these arguments, it's clear that disrupted-time strategies have proved very attractive to female dramatists, and that they have made themselves much more visible – as playwrights – in their work thereby. When, in *Blasted*, a soldier from a Balkan war zone invades a Leeds hotel room, it's clear whose decision we are being invited to judge. It's not the soldier's, it's Sarah Kane's.

In addition to putting the chronologically earliest scene of *Top Girls* at the end of the play, Churchill opens the play with a gathering of successful women, fictional and real, from various incompatible periods of history, connected with the rest of the play neither by plot nor in style but, essentially, by theme. Although – literally – set in the same contemporary world as the rest of the play (and seemingly occurring just before the main course of the play begins), the scene's dramatic thrust is to confront present conditions with comparable or contrasting situations in the past. In doing so, the scene anticipates another structural technique that became very prominent at the close of the last century.

Double and disconnected time

The 1990s trend for plays in which the present investigates the past echoed a development in the novel; this is the structure of Peter Ackroyd's *Hawksmoor* (1985), in which the story of an eighteenth-century architect runs in parallel to events in modern London, and A.S. Byatt's Booker Prize-winning *Possession* (1990), in which a mystery about the life of a Victorian poet is (nearly) unravelled in the present day. One of the earliest stage variants of this pattern is Sarah Woods's 1992 *Nervous Women*, in which a contemporary couple inhabits a room in which a woman was incarcerated as a hysteric a hundred years before. More specifically cast as an exploration of the past, Tom Stoppard's 1993 *Arcadia* is about a contemporary investigation of a past incident in the country house in which the play is set.

Connected by plot, both *Nervous Women* and *Arcadia* not only juxtaposed but also sought to draw comparisons between the two eras. In a stunning *coup de théâtre*, Howard Brenton's earlier *The Romans in Britain* moved from Roman Britain to (then) present-day Northern Ireland at the end of its first act, drawing clear comparisons between the two military occupations. More recently, playwrights have compared eras more elliptically. In both *Handbag* and *Mother Clapp's Molly House*, Mark Ravenhill intercut present-day scenes with scenes set in previous centuries (the era of *The Importance of Being Earnest* and the eighteenth century, respectively). Without any direct plotting connection between the two timescales of

Mother Clapp, Ravenhill foregrounded his own decision to put these two temporally disparate worlds together in the same play; he was directly inviting the audience to compare the worlds of a gay brothel in 1726 and the contemporary London gay scene.

In addition, playwrights have been operating increasingly in disconnected time, putting two or more apparently disparate narratives together and inviting the audience to join up the dots. Bryony Lavery's *Nothing Compares to You* delivers on the traditional promise of this technique: all the apparently unrelated characters in this story of a fatal car crash turn out to be linked to each other (in the final case, by driving the car that caused the accident). In many other recent plays, however, the promise of a literal connection between seemingly inconsonant elements is delivered partially, ambiguously, or not at all. Rebecca Prichard's *Essex Girls* appears initially to be no more than two independent slices of life, the first in a school toilet, the second in the high-rise flat of a beleaguered single mother; the point of the play is to question the connection between the two (whether, for instance, the feisty trio of young women in the first act is set on an inevitable course towards the entrapment of Act 2). David Eldridge's *Under the Blue Sky* consists of three separate duologues: although there is more of a plotting connection between them than in *Essex Girls* (the fate of both of the earlier couples is reported in a later scene), Eldridge's intention is not just that we should follow a narrative, but that we should compare and contrast three relationships. This technique was taken further by Martin Crimp in *Attempts on her Life,* in which a series of apparently disconnected groups and individuals describe what we are invited to think of as a single woman called Anne, possessed nonetheless of various incompatible nationalities, histories and ages, who appears at one point to be a terrorist (of left or right), at another the drowned daughter of grieving parents, at another an artist and even a newly launched car. Crimp's purpose is not only to question whether we can truly know another human being, but whether we can regard other people as existing at all, independent of the models we construct of them. And he achieves this by the dialectical strategy of inviting us to find connections between free-standing scenes, precisely in order to demonstrate that this project is doomed.

A different approach was taken by Simon Stephens in *Pornography*, in which the five separate stories (some in monologue) are linked by the fact that they occurred in the twenty-four hours between London winning the 2012 Olympics and the 7 July bombing attacks on the London Underground in 2005. Stephens invites the director of the play to distribute the lines and order the scenes in any way they like, suggesting that he has abdicated from providing a meaningful connection between them, and that, possibly, he regards them as random.

Pulling the elastic that connects the elements of earlier disrupted- and double-time plays to and beyond the point of snapping, disconnected-time plays have developed a vocabulary of seemingly mundane, often arbitrary connectivity, as a kind of taunting of more conventional, cause-and-effect storytelling. In *The Romans in Britain*, the modern Irish and historical Roman plots are connected archaeologically, by a buried idol. In Anthony Neilson's *Relocated*, the two plots (both fictionalisations of recent murder cases) are linked by hoovering, anagrams, and a piece of cake.

There are a number of reasons why contemporary playwrights – particularly contemporary female playwrights – disrupt conventional, linear time. One of them is a paradox. For thirty years, cultural critics have been proclaiming the decline – if not the death – of traditional linear narrative as a bearer of meaning. In the same period, what's happened in the actual culture is not a rejection or even a problematisation of narrative but a Gadarene rush towards it. In the films, plays and novels of the '70s, narrative is one of a number of means by which writers communicate meaning (along with character, argument and metaphor). By the '90s, the increasing dominance in the electronic media of genre (which, as we've established, means a kind of story) led to narrative becoming the sole bearer of meaning. Despite the work of Stephen Poliakoff and Tony Marchant (and the work of cinema screenwriters like Charlie Kaufman, author of *Eternal Sunshine of the Spotless Mind*), most television drama has long since ceased to problematise, let alone disrupt, linear narrative, as the work of television dramatists like Dennis Potter, Troy Kennedy Martin and Alan Bleasdale did, as a matter of course, in times past.

In addition to everything else they do, plays which disrupt or dislocate time mount a challenge to the overwhelming dominance of narrative in popular drama, and contribute to an extensive canon of work – including many of the plays discussed above – of which the subject is the reliability or otherwise of narrative itself. As we've seen, Sebastian Barry, Tom Stoppard and Michael Frayn have all written plays which dramatise memory. Conor McPherson's *The Weir* is about three men who tell fake ghost stories and a woman who shocks them and us by telling what appears to be a true one. My own play about Hitler's architect and arms minister, *Albert Speer*, sees a man constructing his take on his past life in Act 1, only to have the other characters challenge and undermine it in Act 2. The first scene of Caryl Churchill's *Far Away* consists of a woman trying to explain to a child that the clearly murderous events the child has seen through a window are in fact innocent, constructing a mutating narrative to try to justify each additional and damning piece of evidence. Mark Ravenhill's *Product* consists entirely of a film producer outlining the narrative of a film about a love affair between a Muslim terrorist and his potential victim, squeezing the great issues of our day into the template of a Hollywood movie. The fact that for most of the play we inhabit the producer's narrative – there is nothing outside it or beyond it – makes it both an expression and a critique of the postmodern myth that the text does indeed go all the way down. Martin Crimp's *Fewer Emergencies* also used the format of the pitch to analyse and challenge how we take meaning from story; in his later play *The City* we discover at the end that the play was a fiction written by one of the characters.

Plays which put two or three apparently unrelated narratives together and invite the audience to connect them – as happens in three of Sarah Kane's five plays – are obviously an important part of this canon. Such plays imply or even insist that making cause-and-effect connections is harder than it used to be, but they also assert the overwhelming human urge to do so, however unpropitious the Zeitgeist. As Mark Ravenhill puts it in *Shopping and Fucking*:

> I think... I think we all need stories. We make up stories so we can get by. And I think a long time ago there were big stories. Stories so big you could live your whole life

in them. The Powerful Hands of the Gods and Fate. The Journey to Enlightenment. The March of Socialism. But they all died or the world grew up or grew senile or forgot them, so now we're all making up our own stories. Little stories. But we've each got one.

1. Bertolt Brecht, 'A Short Organum for the Theatre', in *Brecht on Theatre*, trans. John Willett, London: Methuen, 1964, p. 201.

2. See Roger Luckhurst, *The Trauma Question*, London: Routledge, 2008, pp. 179-82.

3. Martin Gottfried, *Arthur Miller: A Life*, London: Faber and Faber, 2003, p. 130.

6
Scenes

Scenes

Earlier, I argued that the action of many plays consists of some kind of promise, prediction, contract or challenge, which is either fulfilled, not fulfilled, or fulfilled in a partial or surprising way.

There is a wonderful short scene in the second episode of Peter Flannery's 1996 BBC2 serial *Our Friends in the North*. It's set in the mid-1960s, in Tosker and Mary's front room in the North-East of England. The marriage is under strain. Tosker wants to be a rock star (and has done a set for a visiting agent); Mary thinks he's having or planning an affair.

MARY. Does she dress up all the time?

TOSKER. Who?

MARY. The one who you were singing to the other night?

TOSKER. What you talking about? What you talking about, woman?

MARY. I'm not blind.

TOSKER. Uh-huh? Well, I'm not blind either.

MARY. Oh, come on, Tosker, you know fine well, Nicky and me...

TOSKER. I don't.

MARY. You do.

TOSKER. I don't.

MARY. Well, you are blind.

TOSKER. What, blind and all, am I? As well as being a tone-deaf brainless shite.

MARY. No one said you were tone-deaf as far as I remember.

TOSKER. Well, you might as well have done.

MARY. Me? I said nothing.

TOSKER. Exactly. You said nothing. I worked my guts out for an hour and a quarter, and you? You say nothing.

MARY. Tosker, I can't be like your mother, telling you lies all the time.

TOSKER. I don't want you to be me mother, I want you to be me wife. A proper wife.

MARY. This phrase. This 'proper wife'.

TOSKER. What do you mean, lies?

MARY. How come we got on to this?

TOSKER. What do you mean, lies?

MARY. Oh, Tosker, man.

TOSKER. All right. All right. Well, you can tell us the truth. Go on.

MARY. I don't want to talk about your act, I want to talk about this woman.

TOSKER. There is no woman, man.

MARY. You're lying.

TOSKER. I'm not lying.

MARY. Okay. I'll tell you the truth if you tell me the truth.

TOSKER. Okay.

MARY. Are you sure?

TOSKER. All right. You go first.

MARY. You can't sing. At least you can't sing any better than half a million other people in the country. You're wasting your time. The agent was right. Sorry.

TOSKER *makes to go.*

Well? Tosker?

TOSKER. There's nobody but you.

What is happening in the scene is a conflict both about and between two questions, each of which is more important to one person than the other. Tosker demands that Mary tell him the truth, and Mary proposes cutting a deal: she'll answer Tosker's question honestly if he answers hers honestly. Tosker agrees, and Mary tells him the truth about his singing, which is what he wants to hear in one sense (it's what she really thinks) but not in another (she thinks he can't sing). Tosker tells her what she wants to hear (he's not being unfaithful); but because the deal has required her to hurt him, she feels embarrassed and ashamed rather than satisfied.

Most of the story of the scene (Mary's growing suspicions, Tosker's gig) has already happened. The plot is the argument (which reveals the matter) and the contract (which resolves it). The action is: 'A woman sets out to discover whether her husband is cheating on her; but pays a price for the discovery.' In the terms I've defined plays, it's a play. Its action is complete.

Except that it isn't. Tosker is lying; he *is* being unfaithful. The action of this scene invites us to believe he's telling the truth; but is contradicted by the wider action of which it is just a part. By presenting an elegant project, followed by a satisfying reversal, Flannery invites us to judge this scene as if it was a whole play. However, the whole scene also serves as a project, to which the rest of the narrative provides a reversal.

Definitions of scenes

Although a complete scene in all these senses, the Mary/Tosker confrontation employs very few of the elements in the scene-writer's armoury. It's a duologue, so no additional characters appear. As both characters are on throughout, there are no comings and goings, except for a small dummy exit at the end. The setting is commonplace and unevocative (both characters know it well, and there's no significant business, beyond Mary's tidying-up of some children's toys). It is also a scene in two senses that are part of the French dramatic vocabulary. The 'French scene' is defined not just by time, place and action, but also by configuration: often set within the same generalised public space, the scene number changes when a character enters or leaves (thus making it an attractive system for stage managers drawing up rehearsal schedules). It's also what the nineteenth-century critic Francisque Sarcey defined as a *scène à faire*, usually translated as an 'obligatory scene': a playing-out of what has become an inevitable confrontation between two characters about the central dramatic questions which divide them ('Ah!', Sarcey exclaims, 'They are going to speak together! What will come of that?').

In our tradition, the scene number changes only when there is a change of time or location. Occasionally, Shakespeare writes scenes in expanded space and time: Act 5 Scene 5 of *Richard III* takes place in Richard and Richmond's tents and in the open space between them; it lasts from nine o'clock in the evening through to and beyond the following dawn. In our own time, there are plays which move between different locations in the same time – Alan Ayckbourn's *Bedroom Farce* is set in three different bedrooms simultaneously – and some which move between different times in the same location – like Ayckbourn's *How the Other Half Loves*, in which two different dinner parties occurring on successive nights are represented concurrently. In my *Testing the Echo*, a dinner party is interrupted by snatches of what the hostess remembers of a difficult meeting which occurred at her workplace earlier the same day. Some one-person plays (like Beckett's *Krapp's Last Tape*) are very specific about their location; others (like Conor McPherson's *St Nicholas*) are performed on an empty stage. Often, plays consisting of consecutive or intercut monologues don't specify a location; though one of the most successful – Brian Friel's *Faith Healer* – describes the settings in some detail. Playwrights can underline the fluidity they want in production by not writing in scene breaks at all (which means that, for rehearsal and technical purposes, someone else will identify them); in Sharman MacDonald's *All Things Nice* the undivided action cuts between scenes in unidentified British locations and spoken letters from one of the character's mothers abroad. In the script of *Fewer Emergencies*, Martin Crimp lists his characters as the numbers 1, 2 or 3, and describes both Time and Place as 'Blank'. But, for all that, even today, the vast majority of stage scenes take place in specified locations, and are consistent in space and time.

If all plays have a story, a plot and an action, then all scenes have a **programme**, a **context**, an **action** and a **situation**.

Elements of scenes

Programme

The programme is not so much a dramaturgical or structural as a logistical tool for the playwright. It's the shopping list of things that a writer needs to get into a scene: the main plot developments, including the introduction of new characters (or all the characters in a first scene), reiterations of names, incidents, and set-ups for developments that will pay off later on. For writers, it's useful to draw up a programme because it prevents things being left out; it also exposes what might be better dealt with in another scene. If a scene turns out to have no programme (or only a small one that could be completed in another scene) it probably shouldn't be there. There is one scene in Shakespeare – the first scene in *Macbeth*, during which the witches make their first appearance – without an exclusive programme: everything we see or learn is repeated when the witches return in the third scene. But the scene is so overwhelmingly powerful, and reveals the tone, character and action of the play so effectively, that its limited programme is trumped by its dramatic effect.

Context

Scenes exist in relation to one another; they begin by answering questions posed in the last scene and often end by propelling the audience into the next one, the technique American script editors call 'topspin'. So, at the beginning of the play scene we know that Hamlet has asked the players to perform a play that will catch the conscience of the king, and that he has asked the leading player to learn a speech of a dozen lines to bring this about. The first speech in the scene, the advice to the players, begins by reminding us of Hamlet's insertion ('Speak the speech, I pray you, as I pronounced it to you'). At the end of the scene, after the play has been performed and interrupted and the king and queen have stormed out, Polonius delivers a summons to Hamlet from his mother to attend on her. Having given more evidence of his derangement to Polonius ('Do you see yonder cloud that's almost in shape of a camel?' he enquires of the ceiling), Hamlet accepts this invitation. Polonius, Rosencrantz and Guildenstern then leave Hamlet to deliver the short soliloquy which closes the scene. The meeting between Hamlet and his mother is discussed in the immediately succeeding scene, and takes place in the one after that. The reminder at the beginning and the set-up at the end are interwoven with other matters of importance, but Shakespeare is careful to make sure we know where we're coming from and where we're going, in a pretty direct and uncluttered way.

In many modern plays, by contrast, the exposition at the beginning of a scene is so considerable that it forms much of its matter. The audience spends the beginning of the second and much of the third act of David Mamet's *Oleanna* working out what's happened in the act breaks. In the first act, we see a university lecturer first ignoring and then hectoring a female student; at the beginning of the second act we learn that, during the passage of time, she has made a complaint about his behaviour; towards the end of the third act we learn that she has accused him of rape in the second break (this information being delayed because she assumes he knows this already). The shift of power from the lecturer to the student is dramatised by his discovering what she's done, before our very eyes.

The scene-break-plotting in Kevin Elyot's three-scene *My Night with Reg* expresses its meaning by wrong-footing the audience. The first scene takes place during the preparation for a dinner party to be attended by a group of gay men, who refer to one of the characters' offstage boyfriend, the Reg of the title. When Scene 2 begins, it appears that the guests have arrived and the dinner party is proceeding (it's still raining). In fact, it's a different rainstorm; time has passed, Reg has died and this is the wake after his funeral, during which several characters reveal having spent their night with Reg and are fearful of having contracted HIV from him. The beginning of the last scene could also be continuous: it is early morning, the rain's still falling, and two characters who don't live in the flat have spent the night there together. However, we find there's been another passage of time, during which Guy, who owns the flat but hasn't spent a night with Reg, has died of AIDS, having contracted HIV during a one-night stand on holiday. So in the first scene break we don't expect a death and one happens; in the second we might expect a death but not the one we get. And therein lies what Elyot wants to say about the seemingly arbitrary nature of the AIDS epidemic and how it felt to be touched or threatened by it.

Similarly, the whole of Scene 7 of Ravenhill's *Shopping and Fucking* consists of the revelation of what's happened since Scene 6. Like the audience, Lulu expects that Robbie has sold three hundred ecstasy tablets – given to him to sell by a dealer – at a rave. The fact that Robbie is in a hospital suggests that all has not gone according to plan. The present-tense action of the scene is Lulu's initially gentle interrogation of Robbie as to why he was mugged and what happened to the drugs. Gradually it emerges that, far from being robbed, Robbie gave away all the tablets on philanthropic grounds ('I felt good, I felt amazing, from just giving, you see?'), and that he was beaten up by the last person to approach him, outraged that he only had two left. Lulu is acutely aware that this puts both of them at extreme risk from the dealer, and, through the early part of the scene, she tenders a number of alternative, more hopeful narratives. By the end she is furious and starts beating up Robbie herself. The scene is about what the play is about: the contestation of narratives.

Scene actions

As I suggested, most scenes contain an action (a project followed by a reversal), which may echo but may also contrast with the action of the play. The action of the play scene in *Hamlet* contributes to the action of the play as a whole: 'Hamlet seeks to prove his uncle's guilt by a device; but his impatience leads him to reveal his hand and places himself and his project in danger.' The action of the hospital scene in *Shopping and Fucking* contrasts with the action of the whole play: Lulu is so angry at Robbie's failure to do what he promised that she nearly abandons her project to provide succour and care for the chaotic men around her. The action of the first act of *Oleanna* ('A college lecturer seeks to reassure an insecure student of her worth, but is too distracted by his own private concerns to notice he's patronising her') explains but also contrasts with the action of the whole play in which the student seeks to destroy the lecturer's career by accusing him of abuse, with the twist that this is a self-fulfilling accusation.

The actions of the three scenes of *My Night with Reg* make the play sound like a comedy of romantic manners. In the first, Guy invites an old university friend for dinner in order to declare his undying love, but finds that the friend has come to cry on Guy's shoulder over his love for Reg. In the second, following Reg's death, Guy tries and fails to declare his love for John a second time; turning to a younger man, Guy finds that Eric, too, is trapped in memories of a past encounter. In the third act, following Guy's death, John is able to acknowledge Guy's love for him at last, but unable to admit his affair with Reg to Reg's lover. But the overall action of the play is not about the wants and desires of the individual characters, but about the way that the AIDS epidemic corrupted the relationships of the whole group, not least by preventing many of those wants and desires being resolved or even expressed. The most poignant line in the last scene of the play is John's: 'He should have said something.'

Situations

The scenes described above are set in a palace, a hospital room, an office, and a flat with sofa and upstage conservatory. Although some plays are set in amorphous or unspecified locations, most scenes have a **situation**, which consists of its **location**, **setting**, **milieu**, **business** and **format**. The location consists not just of the scene's literal and specific stage setting (the kitchen, the general's tent, a patch of grass with a bench), but also its implied surroundings (the central character's house, an army camp, a park). The location will almost certainly suggest a milieu: the world of the family in a private house; the world of administration in an office; the world of exercise in a leisure centre. The setting may lead us to expect certain activities (eating meals in a dining room or a kitchen but less often in a bedroom; holding meetings rather than typing or telephoning in a boardroom). These activities may well involve stage business, from taking a note or lifting a barbell to cooking and eating a meal.

In the same way that a character's role is not necessarily consistent with their rank or office, so activities are not always appropriate to their environment. The telephone brings work into the home, people do their exercises in the dining room, cook in the garden, have sex at the office and eat in bed. One of the nicest moments in Ayckbourn's *Bedroom Farce* is when the oldest of the three couples supplement their earlier, *nouvelle cuisine* dinner with sardines on toast. In a way, the narrower the activity for which the setting is designed, the richer the dramatic potential of something else happening there: hence, in part, the appeal of plays set in lavatories. The first scene of Anthony Minghella's *Made in Bangkok* is set in a baggage-collection hall. In Act 2 of Howard Brenton and David Hare's *Pravda*, business confrontations take place in a private gymnasium, at a race meeting and on a grouse moor. Zoe Lewis set a scene of her *Paradise Syndrome* in a bungee-jumping queue, and, in Howard Brenton's *Weapons of Happiness*, two characters have sex in the London Planetarium.

Choosing an imaginative and unexpected environment for a scene, particularly if it involves evocative business, can draw ironic attention to what's happening. In Nora Ephron's film *When Harry Met Sally*, there's a scene in which Harry and his friend discuss the state of their marriage while watching a football game. The contrast between the intimate, emotional content of their conversation and the public, masculine environment of the ball-game is pointed up during the scene by a Mexican wave, which passes Harry and his friend on three occasions during the scene, and in which they join perfunctorily, without a break in their conversation. Another grouse-shoot (well, strictly, pheasant-shoot) was added to an early scene of Timberlake Wertenbaker's *Our Country's Good*, during which officers of an eighteenth-century Australian penal colony discuss the merits of a harsh punitive policy. Setting a scene which considers executing human beings during a pheasant-shoot had its own resonance, but one potent effect of the situation was to require forceful opinions to be expressed in a whisper. There's a scene in my play *Maydays* in which the protagonist is expelled from a revolutionary party by its leader; the scene was dull until I set it along the 'gauntlet' of revolutionary-newspaper sellers which you have to fight your way through on the way into any left-wing meeting (the papersellers were hawking the imaginary *Workers' Week*, *Revolutionary Worker*, *Revolutionary Marxist Worker* and *Socialist Vanguard*, and the actual *Morning Star*). The way that business can both provide an obstacle and draw attention to the action of a scene is shown in Alan Ayckbourn's *Just Between Ourselves*. The play is about Dennis's failure to understand the emotional needs of the people around him; by setting the play in Dennis's garage, Ayckbourn can dramatise his character's disregard of what others say to him by his aggressive carpentry. In one scene, most of what Dennis's friend Neil is trying to say about his marriage is drowned out by Dennis's electric drill.

And indeed there is one wonderful scene – one of the best Ayckbourn has written – which demonstrates how a well-chosen situation can (in this case, almost literally) electrify a scene. In *A Chorus of Disapproval*, Dafydd is the director of an amateur production of *The Beggar's Opera*. Dafydd's wife Hannah (playing Polly Peachum) is having an affair with Guy (who during the course of the play is promoted from Crook-Finger'd Jack via Matt of the Mint and Filch to MacHeath). Towards the end of the play there is a scene between them in which Guy and Hannah agonise about their situation. During the scene, Hannah has this speech:

> Don't try and pretend to me that you'd consider Dafydd for one single moment if it didn't suit you. It didn't worry you two weeks ago. I would have preferred it if you'd been honest and said another woman, which of course it is. I was prepared to give up everything for you, you know...

That speech and the scene itself work perfectly well. But Ayckbourn had the idea of setting the scene not in a private situation, but in the theatre, just before the costume parade, as director Dafydd is finishing focusing the lights. In the first part of the scene, Guy and Hannah's anguished conversation takes place in a remote corner of the stage, in antiphony, alternating with Dafydd's shouted instructions to Raymond the lighting man (complicated by the fact that Dafydd and Raymond have different lighting plans: 'Could I see your number 18 now, please? That's my number 15, your number 18'). Then, Dafydd decides to drag Hannah and Guy into the lights, as stand-ins for other actors. This is what happens to Hannah's speech:

HANNAH. Don't try and pretend to me that you'd consider Dafydd for one single moment...

DAFYDD (*calling*). I say, you two...

HANNAH. ...if it didn't suit you. It didn't worry you two weeks ago...

DAFYDD (*calling*). I say, you two...

GUY. I think he wants us...

HANNAH (*angrily*). Yes?

DAFYDD (*coming onstage*). Sorry. Were you running lines? Look, just to save time, would you mind standing for me? I just want to check this focus.

He moves GUY *and* HANNAH *into the lights.*

Just move into that one, that's right... Bit further forward, Hannah. Thank you. Just hold it there.

DAFYDD *moves away into the auditorium to check the effect.*

HANNAH (*as she goes, muttering*). Feeblest excuse I have ever heard in my life...

DAFYDD. Hannah, dear, be Annie Anderson for a minute, would you? She's a little taller than you – can you go up on your toes?

HANNAH *goes up on tiptoe.*

Bit more. Thank you.

HANNAH (*awkwardly*). I would have preferred it if you'd been honest and said another woman...

DAFYDD. Guy, my love...

HANNAH. Which, of course, it is.

DAFYDD. Guy, could you go down to Tony Mofitt's size? Would you mind...?

GUY *crouches low.*

GUY. About here?

DAFYDD. Fine. Just hold it. (*He considers for a second.*) No, that's not going to work, Raymond. Show me something else...

During the next, a number of lamps flash on and off the
contorted pair, as RAYMOND *offers* DAFYDD, *who is pacing*
the auditorium, alternative light sources. DAFYDD *rejects*
each in turn.

HANNAH (*on the verge of tears again, softly*). I was
prepared to give up everything for you, you know...

What Ayckbourn is dramatising here is a metaphor: the
betrayed Dafydd throws a spotlight on his wife's infidelity but,
because of his obsession with the show, he can't see what's
literally going on in front of his very eyes. However, the heart of
the scene is the Guy/Hannah conversation, which doesn't need
the lighting plot at all; the scene *could* take place in a dressing
room, or in Guy's flat or in the street. Similarly, in *Weapons of
Happiness*, Janice doesn't have to make her play for Josef Frank
in the Planetarium, nor (in *Pravda*) does Lambert Le Roux need
to humiliate Andrew May on a Yorkshire Moor. Harry's tortured
conversation about his collapsing marriage is enriched by being
punctuated by a Mexican wave (and Neil's by Dennis's drill),
but either could happen on a bus or in the bar.

Formats

Scenarios, ceremonies and roles

There are, however, scenes in which the situation (the location,
its milieu, the associated activity) provides the means by which
the action of the scene is revealed, and without which the scene
couldn't happen at all. In this case, the situation becomes the
scene's **format**. Overwhelmingly, formats are social processes,
ceremonies and rituals which audiences recognise from the real
world, bringing that knowledge with them into the playhouse.
Some formats are very simple (like saying grace or proposing
marriage). Some are hugely complicated, implying not just a
recognised **scenario** of human interaction, but an intricate
matrix of constituent **ceremonies**, **protocols**, **rubrics**,
registers and **roles**. A trial is an obvious example, with its
formalised processes (from the opening statement via
examination of witnesses to the summing-up), its ritualised
procedures (from standing for the entry of the judge to the

passing of the sentence), to its catechisms (from the plea to the verdict) and its many roles (often defined by their location, in the jury box or the dock, on the bench or at the bar). Similarly, a wedding reception implies a number of ceremonial proceedings, several varieties of formalised speaking (from the welcoming line-up to the speeches themselves), and a multiplicity of roles.

While it's possible to imagine a scene in which a wedding reception or the proceedings of a trial were merely the background to an action that could take place somewhere else (in a 2006 television play, Andrew Davies set a love story in and around the jury box of the 1960 Lady Chatterley trial), formats of this complexity almost always enable the action of the scene to unfold. It's obvious that the trial in *The Merchant of Venice* or the three wedding receptions in Richard Curtis's *Four Weddings and a Funeral* enable actions which couldn't be dramatised in any other way. But drama is full of less obvious or complex scenarios, which can be borrowed from life to drive the action of scenes.

In addition to lengthy and elaborate ceremonies (from family reunions to state funerals) there is a repertoire of formats based on various types of formal and informal public gathering. Whether it's the private committee session, the negotiation between two or more opposing delegations, or the public meeting, assemblages of people for public purposes have many common procedures, but also very different dynamics depending on constituency and scale (as is seen in a great meeting scene, the opening of Shakespeare's *Henry VI, Part Two*, which starts with the whole court, narrows down to one faction, and then narrows down again to its leader). Meeting scenes give many examples of the conflict between office, rank, role and character: the low-status chair is bullied by his high-ranking predecessor; the obligatory Silent Person may hold high office (or the Argumentative Person be catapulted from low to high rank by a sudden resignation); the minute-taker ends up making the decisive contribution. In *A Going Concern* and *The Shape of the Table*, Stephen Jeffreys and I set scenes in breakout meetings, the informal caucuses that take place in the next-door room when one faction or another leaves the main meeting for consultations. Even the simplest scenario of human interaction has its roles, rules and complications: in Patrick Marber's *Closer*, Scene 7 is entirely set within a one-to-one conversation in a lap-dancing club, which is certainly a form of human interaction with understood procedures, ritualised behaviours, and particular rules and roles; Scene 3 of the same play consists of an online conversation between two men sitting at computers, one of whom is pretending to be a woman.

A great scene entirely enclosed within a format is the pre-title opening of Anthony Minghella's radio play *Cigarettes and Chocolate*. The scene begins with Gemma's answerphone message and continues with the messages that have been left on the machine during the course of one day. Gemma's callers include Lorna (who wants to go to a movie), Rob (who wants to come round for sex), Alistair (who wants to discourage Gemma from reading a letter he's sent her), Gail (who wants Gemma to help her buy a flat and to accompany her to a hospital appointment), and Gemma's mother (who presumes she's really there). The last three messages in the sequence are from Lorna (desperate, outside the cinema), Rob (leaving his fourth message), and Rob again, sighing. The messages are tremendously eloquent about the people leaving them. Minghella has used recognisable features of answerphone behaviour in order to reveal character (Gail feels rejected when the tape cuts off after thirty seconds; Gemma's irritated mother insists on waiting for Gemma to pick up). But the scene also tells us about Gemma's place in the circle of her acquaintance. Clearly, everyone expects that Gemma will respond immediately to their bidding, and her not doing so is a considerable annoyance and surprise.

We are about to discover that Gemma has decided to stop talking for Lent. As she puts it later (explaining the title):

> Last year it was cigarettes,
> the year before chocolate,
> but this is the best.

This first scene poses a question which that revelation will answer, it introduces us to the characters, and it dramatises an action (a woman whose friends and family rely on her for emotional and practical support surprises them by not responding to their demands), which sets the agenda for the rest of the play. Hannah and Guy's anguished conversation in *A Chorus of Disapproval* would be a lesser scene if it was set in a coffee shop, but it could be. The opening scene of *Cigarettes and Chocolate* could take place nowhere else but on an answerphone.

Smaller formats

The formats in *Cigarettes and Chocolate* and *Closer* define and drive an entire scene. Formats can also propel a section of a scene or a single speech. The mechanicals in *A Midsummer Night's Dream* and Falstaff's potential recruits in *Henry IV, Part Two* are introduced by a roll-call. In David Hare's *A Map of the World*, an altercation between a group of actors about Israel/ Palestine is provoked by an argument about different possible answers to a crossword clue. We learn about the character and politics of the Reverend James Morell in Shaw's *Candida* by the simple expedient of watching him go through his upcoming diary engagements with his secretary: including meetings of the Tower Hamlets Radical Club, the Independent Labour Party, the Hoxton Freedom Group ('Communist Anarchists, I think') and a confirmation class. In all cases, we recognise the rules and roles of a form of human behaviour, from which we are able to draw meaning on the basis of our experience.

A format can provide especial semantic value if its rules and roles are challenged, disrupted or reversed. In Caryl Churchill's *Icecream*, a young woman called Jaq introduces herself to an older woman, Vera, thus:

> Paper round, busker, Tesco, toy factory, jeans shop, Woolworth, winebar, van driver, pavement artist, singer with a rock group, photographer's assistant, office cleaner, primary-school teacher, drug-pusher, vet's receptionist, journalist, cleaning chickens, hospital orderly, gardener, carpenter, my friend's dress shop, traffic warden, tourist guide, hypnotherapist, motorbike messenger, frozen peas, stall in the market, plumber's mate, computer programmer, translator, escapologist, and five secretarial.

Formally, Jaq's speech is a CV. Like any CV, it is intended to impress. But, in this case, what it intends to impress with is not

Jaq's particular skills nor even her breadth of experience but her dizzying professional promiscuity. CVs organise a biography into an attractive narrative by giving its elements priority, hierarchy and chronology. Jaq puts her past jobs in any old order ('paper round, busker, Tesco, toy factory'), she refers to them – seemingly arbitrarily – by position, product and place ('motorbike messenger, frozen peas, stall in the market'), she juxtaposes the admirable with the delinquent ('primary-school teacher, drug-pusher') and she runs out of steam at the end. Jaq's CV tells us a lot about her, but not what a CV is usually designed to convey.

Sarah Woods pulls off a similar trick in the opening speech of *Grace*:

> Tidy room. Hoover. Sort out washing. Fix cupboard door. Put up shelves. Have a child. Make some tea. Get out of bed. Buy: pasta, lettuce, cheese, olives, bread, Ultra Bra, baked beans, washing-up liquid. Cut nails. Eat. Breathe. Get up. Get fit. Learn Russian. Decide what to wear.

Clearly, Grace's speech is a to-do list. But, again, it doesn't fulfil its usual purpose: the point of to-do lists is to bring system and order to chaotic schedules, and this is a wish-list of hard-to-achieve objectives. Grace's seemingly arbitrary, random switching from immediate domestic tasks to huge life choices tells us both about her ambitions (the subject of the play) and the state of mind which provides an obstacle to their fulfilment. Like Jaq's CV, Grace's speech is eloquent, but what it communicates is at odds with what to-do lists are usually designed to do. It's like what happens when you cap a bossy assertion with 'hear, hear!' (implying it sounds like a speech), an argumentative proposal with 'discuss' or a preachy comment with 'amen'. The disruption of our expectations of the register draws attention to the meaning.

Indeed, all of the formats I've described are disrupted in one way or another. For a vicar, the confirmation class should not be crowded out by the Fabian Society. Falstaff's recruits are militarily hopeless (and the only half-good ones merely bribe their way out of service). Bottom misses the point of a casting session, insisting on bidding for every part in *Pyramus and Thisbe*, and challenging Quince for the role of director. In *Much*

Ado About Nothing, Dogberry senses that charges against arraigned persons should be given hierarchy and order, but doesn't entirely succeed:

> Marry, sir, they have committed false report, moreover they have spoken untruths, secondarily they are slanders, sixth and lastly they have belied a lady, thirdly they have verified unjust things, and to conclude, they are lying knaves.

Not all of these disruptions are deliberate (Dogberry is doing his best). But Jaq in *Icecream* knows full well she is flouting the rules, as does the lap-dancer's client in *Closer* when he demands to know her real name. Because we know what should happen during a roll-call or a wedding we immediately recognise – and draw meaning from – any such flouting. A great way of making a scene is to make a scene.

Formats in action

Though it's hard to think of a play which doesn't evoke and manipulate some recognisable protocol or ritual at some point, few plays are entirely contained within a format, and sensible playwrights balance formatted scenes with scenes in which the characters aren't bound by ceremonial etiquette, and can speak and behave freely. Many Shakespeare scenes employ formats, but he rations them (in *Hamlet*, they are the court scene, the play scene, Ophelia's funeral and the duel at the end). It's worth looking at three examples of disrupted Shakespearian formats, of differing complexity, scale (how much of the scene operates within the format), and balance (between the format and its disruption).

Act 3 Scene 2 of *The Winter's Tale* is set in the court of Leontes, King of Sicily, who has arraigned his wife Hermione for adultery with his friend Polixenes and conspiracy with a disgraced councillor, Camillo. Leontes has already sent Hermione's baby daughter – which he thinks was fathered by Polixenes – to 'some remote and desert place', where, Oedipus-like, 'chance may nurse or end it'. After the charges are read, Hermione tries to answer them, but is harried by Leontes. Then two courtiers, who have returned from Apollo's shrine at Delphos, reveal the god's judgement:

> Hermione is chaste, Polixenes blameless, Camillo a true subject, Leontes a jealous tyrant, his innocent babe truly begotten, and the king shall live without an heir if that which is lost be not found.

Following this unambiguous judgement, news arrives that Leontes and Hermione's older child has died through fear for his mother's fate, and Hermione herself collapses, as if dead. Leontes realises his error and resolves to mourn his wife and child for the rest of his life. The action of the scene is: 'A king mounts a show-trial to prove his queen guilty of adultery, but finds out that he is guilty of paranoia.' The trial format not only allows for accusation (the project of the scene) but its reversal, when unexpected evidence leads to the collapse not just of the case but of the court. So the format's structure reflects that of the action: a project followed by a reversal. And in this case the disruption of the ritual brings about a redistribution of its constituent roles: Leontes starts out as a prosecutor posing as a judge, and ends up in the dock.

The whole of this scene is set within the format of the trial. By contrast, the first scene of *King Lear* demonstrates how a scene's agenda can be revealed by the disruption of a small and simple format, completed in a fraction of its length. The programme of the scene is vast: the territory to be covered including Lear's abdication, the elevation of Goneril and Regan, the abandonment of Cordelia by one of her suitors, her exile and Kent's banishment (there is also a brief set-up of the parallel plot of Gloucester and his sons Edgar and Edmund). The action of the scene is: 'An abdicating king seeks to discover which daughter most deserves his favour, but picks wrongly.' The format is a simple test, which we don't necessarily recognise, but don't need to, because its rules are clear: each daughter has to declare her love for her father, each one outdoing the previous one (in production, the test can be played as a regular pastime, or a new invention). Cordelia refuses to play the game by the rules, thus provoking Lear to take the actions that will ultimately destroy him.

Most but not all of Act 3 Scene 4 of *Macbeth* consists of the state banquet disrupted by the appearance of Banquo's ghost. But, unlike in *The Winter's Tale* and *King Lear*, the format is disrupted pretty much from the start. Hardly has Macbeth sat his guests down, and announced his *faux*-democratic decision to sit among them, than one of his murderers appears with news that they've killed Banquo but not his son. Less than ten lines after the murderer goes, Banquo's Ghost appears to shake his 'gory locks' at the usurper. The ceremonial aspect of the event is important: Lady Macbeth says that 'meeting were bare without it', and spends much of the scene trying to rescue the party. The banquet is there to provide an audience for Macbeth's guilty anguish. In *The Winter's Tale* and *King Lear* the reversal takes place within the format. Here, it works against it. The action of the scene – 'Macbeth seeks to enjoy his kingship, but his guilt at Banquo's murder demonstrates he will never feel safe' – is all about the protagonist.

In each of these cases, the disruption of the format (the trial, the test, the banquet) expresses the scene's meaning.

I have, of course, chosen examples which are frequently used in drama. Tests of various sorts occur frequently in Shakespeare and persist in Brecht (in *The Caucasian Chalk Circle*, it provides the title). Lear's test of his daughters is a kind of game; most of the second half of Patrick Marber's *Dealer's Choice* consists of a poker game, during which conflicts established in Act 1 are played out and resolved across a card table. Chekhov's *The Seagull*, Arnold Wesker's *Chicken Soup with Barley* and Charlotte Keatley's *My Mother Said I Never Should* all involve card games in their last act. Disrupted trials pepper Shakespeare and define a genre of twentieth-century drama. Difficult meals run from *Macbeth* and *Timon of Athens* via *The Importance of Being Earnest* to Howard Brenton's *The Genius*. Timon serves his guests stones; Cecily forces cake and sugared tea on Gwendolen; Brenton's eponymous physicist hands out urine instead of champagne at a university drinks party.

Another play from the early 1980s sets a format inside a situation which doesn't necessarily imply it. Set in early-nineteenth-century Ireland, Brian Friel's *Translations* contains a scene in which a group of British Army officers are explaining to what is, in effect, a public meeting of Gaelic-speaking

Irishmen and women that they are surveying the area. The scene includes a number of important set-ups – including the fact that the British plan to 'standardise' the place names of the region – but its main purpose is to show the British Army attempting to sell what they describe as a benign process of rationalisation, but which the locals regard as an act of colonial interference. Although it could be dramatised in a different way, this action is revealed through the format of translation, enabled by the fact that both English and Gaelic are rendered in English, so we can hear both the original English of Captain Lancey's pitch and the content of his co-lingual interpreter's subtle adaptation, intended both to clarify the Captain's content and to mollify his listeners. So Captain Lancey's 'general triangulation which will embrace detailed hydro-graphic and topographical information' becomes 'a new map', and 'the present survey has for its object the relief which can be afforded to the proprietors and occupiers of land from unequal taxation' is translated as 'the new map will mean that taxes are reduced'. At the end, Captain Lancey assures his listeners that Ireland is privileged by the survey; while his interpreter suggests that the undertaking demonstrates the Government's interest in Ireland, and thanks the audience for its attentive listening.

So, in *Translations*, one format (the public meeting) encases another (translation). Another play where formats are encased by distinct situations is Act 3 of Rostand's *Cyrano de Bergerac*. The action of the play is that the brilliant but nasally overendowed Cyrano loves the beauteous Roxanne, who ought to love him, but loves the dim-witted but dashing Christian instead. Allowing his love for Roxanne to overwhelm his own interests, Cyrano has drafted Christian's love letters for him, but now Roxanne has demanded that Christian express his passion in person, which he signally fails to do. To rescue the situation, Christian stands beneath Roxanne's window on a dark night and, first rehearsed and then prompted by the hidden Cyrano, declares his love with all the poetic passion of the letters. However, when Roxanne comments on Christian's halting delivery, Cyrano takes over, speaking 'in an approximation of Christian's voice', eventually persuading Roxanne to allow her lover to climb up a nearby tree and kiss her.

This looks like a balcony scene, a simple format in which men declare love for women upwards at night, in this case disrupted by the fact that the declarer is actually somebody else. But, in fact, the balcony merely provides the background situation against which the real driver of the scene can operate, which is that Cyrano is speaking to the woman he loves on behalf of his rival. The distinction is well demonstrated by the (frequent) occasions in which film-makers have transplanted the device into different milieus. In James L. Brooks's *Broadcast News*, for example, ambitious television news-editor Jane admires her homely but talented colleague Aaron, while nursing a secret yearning for attractive newcomer Tom. When Jane is asked to produce a news special about a Libyan bombing attack, Tom is chosen over Aaron to front the broadcast and thus to conduct interviews with other reporters as Jane feeds him questions through his earpiece. Disconsolately watching the broadcast at home, Aaron phones Jane, suggesting the questions and comments which she should propose to Tom, transforming the quality of the broadcast ('I say it here,' murmurs Aaron in wonderment, 'it comes out there'). There are differences between this situation and Act 3 of *Cyrano*: notably that the woman knows what's happening and the helped man doesn't. But they share the basic geometry, and the mechanism whereby that geometry is dramatised and changed. In both cases, a lover is helping a rival by prompting.

It's no surprise that, like this one, so many formats are metatheatrical. Shakespeare was aware of the power of theatre both to advance a project (such as exposing your uncle as a murderer) and to provide that project's reversal (*Hamlet* is one of three Shakespeare plays in which an onstage audience disrupts a play-within-a-play, the others being *Love's Labour's Lost* and *A Midsummer Night's Dream*). Chekhov consciously borrowed the idea of an author interrupting his own play in *The Seagull*; the action of the first act is: 'A young man seeks to impress his mother, her lover and the woman he himself loves by presenting a play to the first two performed by the third; the failure of the play widens the gulf with his mother and threatens his relationship with the woman.' Like Shakespeare, many writers have appreciated the power of preparatory theatrical formats (notably rehearsals) in communicating meaning. Playwrights from Shakespeare via Jean Anouilh to Timberlake Wertenbaker have used theatrical formats several times in the same play, thickening their meaning and resonance as they go.

Compounds and complications

When Max Stafford-Clark chose to pair George Farquhar's 1706 masterpiece *The Recruiting Officer* with Timberlake Wertenbaker's 1988 adaptation of Thomas Keneally's *The Playmaker, Our Country's Good*, the reason was that the Keneally novel is about a performance of the Farquhar play by convicts in the Australian penal colony in 1789. But the similarities of the plays don't end with subject matter: there are formal links as well.

Both plays take a connected set of scenarios and use them as a series of formats for the central scenes of the play. In *The Recruiting Officer* the formats are various forms of military recruitment. On the first two occasions when we see conscription in action, in Sergeant Kite's initial announcement of his presence and purpose in Shrewsbury town square and the recruitment of two men in Act 2 Scene 3, we are in the recognisable territory of grand rhetoric, intoxication, soft recruiters and hard recruiters, and the discovery of monarchical shillings. By Act 3 Scene 1, in which Sergeant Kite tries to press the bucolic Bullock into service while his captain tries to 'press' his sister's chickens, the format is already beginning to pun: 'recruiting' is taking on a sexual meaning. This coding of recruitment as a form of seduction prepares us for the pivotal Act 3 Scene 2, one of those wonderful Restoration scenes in which the playwright brings everybody together out of doors. In this case, Farquhar brings all the major characters together except one, Plume's inamorata Sylvia, who has disappeared off into the country in Act 2, murmuring lightly (if our memory is that acute) of her tiredness of petticoats. She reappears dressed as a man, provoking an unseemly contest between the two recruiting officers – Plume and Brazen – for her commitment to their colours. We know why this young man is so intriguingly appealing to them, but they don't. By Act 4 the recruitment/seduction pun is driving the plot, as Sergeant Kite, disguised as a fortune-teller, demonstrates on military recruits the trick he will use – later in the same scene – to secure the Lady Melinda for Mr Worthy (his trick is to know in disguise about things he has himself done out of it, and to appear to predict happenings he will himself bring about). It's worth noting that Sergeant Kite has already used prediction of the future, in the metatheatrical form of role-play ('You're a justice of peace, and you're a king, and I'm a duke') in his recruiting pitch to Coster Pearmain and Thomas Appletree back in Act 2.

Timberlake Wertenbaker chose to use the same mechanism in *Our Country's Good*. There are eight scenes in the play set within theatrical formats: the audition, a scene in which the script is being written out, two scenes in which characters are learning their lines, three major rehearsals, and the planning of the curtain call just before the first performance actually begins (at the very end of Wertenbaker's play). All of these scenes reveal what is happening between the characters through their efforts to suppress the reality of their situation under the formality of the theatrical procedures.

Wertenbaker is not the first (nor the last) person to realise the peculiar dramatic character of the theatrical audition. In auditions for the part of Hitler in Mel Brooks's 1968 film *The Producers* and for membership of a Dublin soul band in Dick Clement, Ian La Frenais and Roddy Doyle's *The Commitments*, the dominant characters are the auditionees, none of whom (in either film) are we ever going to see again. In both cases, the real central characters are the largely silent auditioners, and the valuable dramatic information is not the performances but their response to them (in *The Commitments*, cigarette-drooping incredulity; in *The Producers*, the persistent, interruptive cry of 'Next!'). It's the expectation that audition scenes fail which, initially, propels the audition scene in *The Full Monty*, in which a group of redundant Sheffield workers are trying to recruit a male stripping troupe in a grimy abandoned warehouse. The first audition fulfils our expectations by being an embarrassing disaster; the second appears to be heading in the same direction when the performer reveals an unanticipated skill (although in his fifties, he's still a nifty dancer); the third audition follows the same pattern (though the 'skill' here is the auditionee's enormous sexual equipment). So, in this case, the action is the expectation of failure, and the reversal an unforeseen success: 'Despite everything working against it, the group nonetheless succeeds in recruiting the new members it needs.' As a result, the scene not only tells us about the people doing the auditioning, but also introduces two new members of the team. In this, *The Full Monty* joins other great team-gathering narratives, from *The Wizard of Oz* to *The Magnificent Seven*.

The audition scene in *Our Country's Good* follows this pattern. Wertenbaker uses the audition format to introduce the convicts and dramatise the contrast between their lives, the subject matter of the play-within-the-play and indeed the normal business of playmaking. The first auditionee is Meg Long, who has taken literally the news that Second Lieutenant Ralph Clark (the army officer who's directing the play) is looking for some women. The second is Robert Sideway, a pickpocket who has clearly always nursed theatrical ambitions. The third is a pair: the pushy Dabby Bryant, who wants the parts being offered to the silent Mary Brenham. Last is Liz Morden, whose particular problem with being cast in the play (she will be sentenced to hang before the first night) will dominate rehearsals. In their different ways, all of the auditionees disrupt the process: by refusing to understand the fictional nature of the play, or insisting on reversing roles, so that they are auditioning the director. The last line of the scene is Liz Morden's 'I'll look at it and let you know.'

During the rehearsal scenes of *Our Country's Good*, the plausibility of Farquhar's play is challenged by convicts whose life experience is different from the characters'; actors refuse to say lines, demand recasting, and boycott scenes which involve the colony's hangman. Two of the rehearsals are interrupted by the military police, and, in one, actors are forced to rehearse in chains. There is also a powerful scene which starts in a theatrical format but shifts into another. On the beach at night, Mary Brenham rehearses her lines (in Sylvia's male costume). Ralph enters and, as Captain Plume, gives Mary her cues. Gradually, however, Farquhar's lines ('Will you lodge at my quarters in the meantime?') take on a present-tense significance: Ralph is seducing Mary. As in *The Recruiting Officer* with recruitment, so in *Our Country's Good* the act of rehearsal is encoded sexually. Its new coding can then be reactivated, with that resonance built in, whenever the playwright wishes. As, in Noël Coward's *Present Laughter*, Garry Essendine seduces Joanna through a discussion of London concert halls, so – in *Still Life/Brief Encounter* – Alec and Laura both evade and express their impermissible passion by discussing preventive medicine ('You were saying about the coal mines...'). In John Osborne's screen adaptation of *Tom Jones*, one of Tom's conquests is achieved through the increasingly lascivious – and wordless – eating of a meal.

But the best example of the way in which a performance format exposes a subtext comes from one of the greatest dramatic scenes ever written, the first tavern scene in *Henry IV, Part One*. The scene has two contexts. We know that the roistering Prince Hal plans to throw off his rude associates eventually ('redeeming time when men least think I will'). More immediately, we've seen him play a joke on Sir John Falstaff and his associates: expecting help from the prince and his sidekick Poins, the gang has robbed a group of pilgrims on a country road and been robbed in turn (in fact, by Hal and Poins, disguised in buckram cloaks). Act 2 Scene 4 takes place back at the hideout; in this case, The Boar's Tavern at Eastcheap, where Team Falstaff has agreed to meet and share the spoils.

The scene has a five-part structure. Like many Chekhov scenes it starts and ends with a duologue, ballooning in the middle. The first section sets up the agenda for the scene by showing Prince Hal abusing his status and mounting a trick: he tries to persuade the tavern's lowly drawer Francis into leaving his job, a situation complicated by Ned Poins, from off, calling out for service, provoking Francis's repeated call: 'Anon anon, sir.' This jape is interrupted by the arrival of Falstaff, who has – he thinks – been betrayed by Hal and Poins's failure to join him in the robbery. To explain losing the stolen money, Falstaff then constructs an elaborate fantasy of how he fought off an escalating number of men in buckram green, which is finally punctured by Hal, who reveals that the (by now) eleven men in green were in fact two – Hal and Poins themselves, who robbed the robbers. The scene is interrupted a second time by what we might think to be the police, but is in fact a messenger calling Hal back to London to see his father the king, and to prepare for war against the rebels in the North. A little later, the authorities do indeed arrive – the third interruption in the scene – and Hal uses his position to resolve the robbery question before departing for the court.

Between interruptions two and three comes a scene of awesome dramatic power, in which Falstaff and Hal rehearse what Hal should say to the king, in justification of his behaviour. Initially, Falstaff plays the king, in which role he instructs his 'son' to abandon all his low associates except for one – the only virtuous man in Hal's company, whose name for the moment escapes him. Outraged by this special pleading, Hal insists that he and Falstaff swap roles, so that Falstaff plays Hal, and Hal his father. Once again, Falstaff uses the situation to plead for himself, begging the king to banish Peto, Bardolph and Poins, but 'for sweet Jack Falstaff, kind Jack Falstaff, true Jack Falstaff, valiant Jack Falstaff, and therefore more valiant being, as he is, old Jack Falstaff, banish not him thy Harry's company, banish not him thy Harry's company. Banish plump Jack and banish all the world'. To which the prince replies, as his father, 'I do', and, as himself, 'I will'.

Just look at what's happening here. In what is – in format terms – an improvised role-play, Falstaff the false father plays the true father and instructs the actual son not to spurn him, provoking laughter thereby. Then, playing the true son, he argues to the actual son (playing the true father) that he (the father) shouldn't banish him – which, because it is a repeat in a different form of the previous joke, we laugh at, until we realise what the underlying situation has become: not that the false father as the true son is pleading with the true father, but that the false father is pleading directly with the true son. So as (in *Our Country's Good*) a stage seduction becomes a real seduction, so in this devastating scene a stage plea becomes a real plea, which is rejected first in role and then for real.

In the chapter on Character, I argued that characters are often revealed most clearly when they are wearing a mask: in this case, the mask Falstaff is wearing is of the man in front of him. In the same way that the geometry of the *Cyrano* balcony scene is replicated in *Broadcast News*, so the mechanism of the tavern scene has been reproduced in other plays. In my *Destiny*, two members of the neofascist National Forward party fire hostile questions at their party's candidate in a parliamentary by-election; gradually it becomes clear that, though pretending to be opponents of their party in order to prepare their candidate, they are using the exercise to battle with each other for the party's soul. The *Henry IV, Part One* tavern scene is even more directly echoed in Scene 4 of April de Angelis' *The Positive Hour*, set in a group-therapy session which is discussing student Nicola's difficulties in resisting pressure from a demanding father to stay with him at home. First time round, Nicola plays herself and another member of the group plays her father (not very well), and Nicola succeeds in getting out of the house and to her college class. But then the group leader suggests they swap, so that Nicola plays her father. Suddenly Nicola is animated and empowered; through her bitter, sarcastic portrayal of her father we see her own pent-up energies released; we learn not just what he's like but what she could be if she broke free of him.

There's another scene – this time in a movie – in which one person plays a hostile other, thereby revealing a truth about himself. In *Citizen Kane*, the fiery, radical young newspaper owner pledges himself to the highest principles of honesty and integrity, which are shared by his friend and helpmeet Jedediah Leland. Over the years, as Kane increasingly abandons his youthful ideals, the two men drift apart, and Leland ends up as drama critic on Kane's Chicago paper.

Later, Kane marries a cabaret singer and decides to turn her into an opera star. After a (disastrous) first night in the Chicago opera house he has built for her, Kane goes to his newspaper office, where Leland is supposed to be reviewing the opera. In fact, the drunk Leland has started what is clearly going to be a stinker, but fallen asleep over the typewriter. Kane arrives at the office, reads the vituperative first paragraph ('Miss Susan Alexander, a pretty but hopelessly incompetent amateur...'), demands that he be brought another typewriter, and finishes the review. Leland wakes, picks up the situation, assumes Kane is changing the review's conclusions, but is told that Kane is finishing it exactly the way Leland started it, as a viciously hostile notice. When Kane greets him, Leland says, 'I didn't know we were speaking', and Kane responds, 'Sure we're speaking, Jedediah – you're fired.'

Formats, situations and obligatory scenes

The opera-review scene in *Citizen Kane* is an obligatory scene, in that it's the confrontation between two characters which we've been waiting for. Often, the obligatory confrontation between two contending forces in the play involves clearing the stage and leaving them to it. But occasionally, as in *Kane*, an effective format can provide a complication which intensifies the encounter.

In another case, the format of one obligatory moment provides the situation for another. In what is structurally the subplot of *Much Ado About Nothing*, Beatrice and Benedick have pledged never to fall victim to romance, particularly with each other. Their friends decide to convince these two combatants that they are in love, by contriving that Benedick and Beatrice each overhear discussions to this effect.

From the moment Beatrice hears that Benedick loves her, we're waiting for the obligatory moment when the two of them will next meet alone. Shakespeare does two things to increase the power of their encounter. First he delays it, through much of the complicating action of the 'main' plot, in which the villainous Don John persuades Benedick's friend Claudio that his fiancée, Beatrice's cousin Hero, is unfaithful. The obligatory culmination of this plot is Claudio and Hero's wedding scene, interrupted by Claudio charging Hero with infidelity, as a result of which Hero faints and is borne off, presumed dead. Thus far we are in a classic disrupted ceremony: the format is the marriage service, the reversal Claudio's accusation.

Now the church provides an extremely evocative location for what happens next. Claudio's best friend Benedick and Hero's cousin Beatrice are both present at the wedding, and are left alone (at last) after the other protagonists depart. At the beginning of their scene together, Beatrice tells Benedick she wants him to fulfil a task, he asks what it is, and she has nearly told him when he interrupts her, protesting his love. Beatrice responds by declaring her love for him, whereupon Benedick returns the conversation to its original topic by asking what task she has for him. Her reply is: 'Kill Claudio.'

The obligatory (and predictable) moment – which we might expect to be one of high comedy – is thus placed within the context of another important turning point, and transformed.

In a final twist, Shakespeare echoes his dovetailing of the two plots in another obligatory scene. Benedick's friends wanted him to fall for Beatrice in order to see him renege on his promise never to fall in love. We have thus been anticipating the moment when Benedick's friends Don Pedro and Claudio will have the chance of crowing over the breaking of Benedick's pledge, almost as eagerly as the predicted love scene itself. Since Beatrice's injunction, we have wondered whether Benedick can issue a challenge to his friend. Shakespeare has so engineered it that these two expectations must be fulfilled in the same scene, so Claudio expects to have a good comic crow but in fact receives a far from comic challenge. The culmination of the comic jape (the pretend romance of Benedick and Beatrice) is trumped by the consequence of the tragic jape (the pretend infidelity of Hero).

Why formats matter

As I've said, few plays operate entirely within a format, and even Shakespeare rations them carefully. Brecht places lots of his scenes within recognisable formats, though never all of them, and Chekhov sets many of his scenes against ceremonies of various kinds (from performances to parties). Ibsen uses them very sparingly; but when they do happen – as when Nora's rehearsal of the tarantella gets out of hand in *A Doll's House* – they are particularly powerful as a result.

So why do they matter so much? There are three reasons. Usually, formats employ scenarios that audiences recognise, and thus, like genres, arrive onstage fully equipped with expectation, and ready-primed to be blown apart. Second, as we've seen, they provide a multiplicity of performative roles against which characters can revolt.

But, third, ceremonies matter to us as audiences because they matter to us as people. Almost all of us participate in some kind of ceremony pretty much every day. The great moments of our lives are marked by them, and our sense of identity (as members of a family, a community, a religion, a country or a species) is defined by them. They express our human urge to gather, to ritualise, to perform, to commemorate, to solemnise and to repeat. They make things grand and they make things strange.

If lyric poetry inhabits the individual feeling and the novel the individual thought, then drama confronts our private dreams and agonies with the public rituals designed to mark and come to terms with them. The disruption of the wedding or the funeral, the trial or rite, the feast or festival, is an expression of our failure fully to accept the sometimes bitter truths they signify. They make great drama because they are great drama.

7
Devices

Devices

Act 2 of Terence Rattigan's *The Winslow Boy* ends with a noted *coup de théâtre*. The son of Arthur Winslow has been accused of stealing a postal order from a fellow pupil at his naval boarding school, and is expelled. His father believes that the boy is innocent and, through his solicitor Desmond Curry, invites a leading barrister – and Member of Parliament – to prosecute the case against the Admiralty in court. On his way to a grand dinner, Sir Robert Morton comes round to talk to Ronnie Winslow, in order to decide whether to take the case. He insists the family stays to witness the interview with young Ronnie, but requires them to remain silent.

The interview starts quietly, but it is quickly clear that Morton aims to unpick Ronnie's case. He forces Ronnie to admit that he knew how the boy who lost the postal order wrote his signature, and wrote it that way when asked to do so after the order was lost:

> SIR ROBERT. When you wrote on the envelope, what made you choose that particular form?
>
> RONNIE. That was the way he usually signed his name –
>
> SIR ROBERT. How did you know?
>
> RONNIE. Well – he was a great friend of mine –
>
> SIR ROBERT. That is no answer. How did you know?
>
> RONNIE. I'd seen him sign things.
>
> SIR ROBERT. What things?
>
> RONNIE. Oh – ordinary things.
>
> SIR ROBERT. I repeat: what things?
>
> RONNIE (*reluctantly*). Bits of paper.

SIR ROBERT. Bits of paper? And why did he sign his name on bits of paper?

RONNIE. I don't know.

Having established that Ronnie had practised writing/forging his friend's signature, Morton pulls his alibi apart. Pressed on what he was doing for the twenty-five minutes during which he could have stolen the postal order, Ronnie prevaricates:

RONNIE. Perhaps I waited outside the C.O.'s office.

SIR ROBERT (*with searing sarcasm*). Perhaps you waited outside the C.O.'s office! And perhaps no one saw you there either?

RONNIE. No. I don't think they did.

SIR ROBERT. What were you thinking about outside the C.O.'s office for twenty-five minutes?

RONNIE (*wildly*). I don't even know if I was there. I can't remember. Perhaps I wasn't there at all.

SIR ROBERT. No. Perhaps you were still in the locker-room rifling Elliot's locker –

ARTHUR (*indignantly*). Sir Robert, I must ask you –

SIR ROBERT. Quiet!

RONNIE. I remember now. I remember. Someone did see me outside the C.O.'s office. A chap called Casey. I remember I spoke to him.

SIR ROBERT. What did you say?

RONNIE. I said: 'Come down to the Post Office with me. I'm going to cash a postal order.'

SIR ROBERT (*triumphantly*). *Cash* a postal order.

RONNIE. I meant get.

SIR ROBERT. You said cash. Why did you say cash if you meant get?

RONNIE. I don't know.

SIR ROBERT. I suggest cash was the truth.

RONNIE. No, no. It wasn't. It wasn't really. You're muddling me.

SIR ROBERT. You seem easily muddled. How many other lies have you told?

As Ronnie's case collapses, his family intervenes to try and protect him. Remorselessly, Sir Robert Morton accuses Ronnie of being a forger, a liar and a thief. As Ronnie weeps on his mother's breast, Morton turns to Desmond the solicitor:

> SIR ROBERT (*to* DESMOND). Can I drop you anywhere? My car is at the door.
>
> DESMOND. Er – no – I thank you –
>
> SIR ROBERT (*carelessly*). Well, send all this stuff round to my chambers tomorrow morning, will you?
>
> DESMOND. But – but will you need it now?
>
> SIR ROBERT. Oh, yes. The boy is plainly innocent. I accept the brief.
>
> *He bows to* ARTHUR *and* CATHERINE, *and walks languidly to the door, past the bewildered* JOHN, *to whom he gives a polite nod as he goes out.* RONNIE *continues to sob hysterically.*

The format of this scene is a simulated cross-examination. Revealed only at its climax, its action is: 'By apparently exposing his guilt, a lawyer convinces himself of his client's innocence' (he explains the reasons for his volte-face – that Ronnie made too many admissions, evaded a trap, and failed to make use of an offered loophole – early in the next act). But the scene also contains a multitude of devices. They include the **configuration** (who's onstage), an **injunction** (the command to the family not to interrupt) and its inevitable **violation**. In the cross-examination, key words are repeated in different contexts (in the sections quoted they include 'things', 'bits of paper', 'outside the C.O.'s office', 'perhaps', 'cash' and 'muddled'). A sense of urgency is provided by the dinner Morton has to go to (of which we are constantly reminded by his evening dress). The scene builds slowly to a dramatic climax, which is followed by a short, brisk and unexpected reversal. Many scenes contain some of the above devices, but few contain them all.

Devices are mechanisms for conveying dramatic meaning within scenes (and, sometimes, between them). It might seem that in discussing them I've reached the bottom of the playwright's toolkit. This is true in the sense that devices work in the same way as scenes work and whole plays work, only in miniature. But the device goes to the very heart of what the theatre is.

Some (though not all) devices seek to confront what looks like theatre's biggest problem: its difficulty in showing what goes on inside people's heads, the thing that novels do so effortlessly. For this reason we often think of the devices that the theatre has developed to show what it cannot show directly – the chorus, the aside, the soliloquy, the ghost and the alter ego – as being like a repair kit, a set of crude fixatives to patch up the mechanical failures of the medium.

Increasingly, I think this is quite wrong, and that these devices are at the core of the art. In the same way that the starting point of figurative painting is the techniques by which you render three dimensions in two, so the whole point of the theatre is to make the invisible visible by finding ingenious ways to expose it, in devices which almost always involve sharing something – a convention, a code – with the audience.

When the Chorus in *Henry V* implores the audience, 'Think, when we talk of horses, that you see them', it is not an apology for lack of resources. It is an invitation to join in.

Dialogue

Most of the devices I want to talk about are expressed in dialogue, the basic building block of most plays. The playwright and teacher Michelene Wandor argues compellingly that dialogue is 'the *only* significant (and signifying) literary means whereby the dramatic text can be imagined and written'.[1] You don't have to agree with that completely to acknowledge that dialogue is a great deal more than the icing on the cake. There are some basic dialogue rules which it's worth mentioning at the outset.

The first is that dialogue is just that: a spoken exchange. It's a good principle to make sure that no line of dialogue would be like it is without the preceding lines. There are exceptions: people sometimes do know what they're going to say in advance, and ride roughshod over any interruption; certainly, we skip, referring back to something that was said earlier by us ('And another thing...') or by someone else ('What do you mean, grumpy?'). But by and large, if line C isn't provoked by line B (or an earlier line A) then one of them needn't be there.

That said, it's worth remembering that we all put a certain amount of what linguists call 'redundancy' into what we say, partly so we can work out what we want to say next (the politician's throat-clearing 'I'm glad you asked me that question'), but also so our listeners can catch up with the meat of what we're trying to communicate. Steve Gooch is correct to advocate 'weeding', snipping out the 'wells', 'whats', 'anyways', 'justs' and 'you knows' with which normal speech is peppered, as well as feed-lines like 'Continue', 'Go on', 'Really?' and 'Oh?'[2] Later on I argue that, in a certain kind of dialogue, eliminating that redundancy exposes meaning that would otherwise be smothered. But, a word of caution: like any other listener, audiences need to process what they're hearing, and the occasional, semantically redundant phrase allows them to do so. A redundant phrase can tell us about the speaker or the listener: an example is Jorgen Tesman's irritating trope in *Hedda Gabler* (usually translated as 'Think of that', or 'Fancy that', but very effectively rendered as 'Amazing' in Richard Eyre's 2005 translation for the Almeida Theatre). The interpolation of prompting 'Continues' and 'Go ons' are certainly signs of lazy playwriting, but people do stop in mid-flow, for dramatic effect, to check whether the listener is following, or for fear that they've gone too far. And, certainly, we indulge in 'phatic speech', saying things not to communicate meaning but to keep the conversation going. The novelist David Lodge points out that almost the whole of Harold Pinter's sketch *Last to Go* is 'mutually and simultaneously phatic for *both* interlocutors, maintaining contact but not conveying much information between them. This accounts for the extraordinary amount of repetition in the dialogue.'[3]

Phatic speech is an example of what linguists call 'infelicitous speech acts', sayings which don't fulfil the conditions of a valid statement effectively communicated. These conditions include the context of the speech (the speaker must be authorised to perform the act undertaken in the speech, have evidence for its content, and, if the act is a question, be ignorant of the answer), its sincerity (the speaker must mean what he says, believe it to be true and genuinely want the answer), and the speech must be 'essential' in the sense that the speaker is obliged to make it. The listener must recognise the first speaker's intentions, and take the speech act in the spirit in which it was formed (distinguishing between an observation and a warning, for instance).[4]

It's clear that most statements made in the world – and almost all statements made in plays – are infelicitous speech acts in at least one of these senses, and their infelicity communicates their meaning. Judgements are made by unauthorised persons, questions are asked to which the speaker knows the answer, people lie, say things they don't mean, don't mean to say, or don't have to say in the first place. Listeners are worse, misunderstanding what is being said to them or not listening at all. Early on in *Much Ado About Nothing*, Beatrice makes this very point to Benedick: 'I wonder that you will still be talking, Signor Benedick. Nobody marks you.' Often, an encoded remark is read literally, or vice versa. Throughout the first act of *Oleanna*, the lecturer is saying things in one form which are received in another (later, the student will challenge his claim that his statements 'mean what you *said* they meant'). In *My Night with Reg*, when John tells Guy that he's 'the only one...', Guy doesn't realise this sentence will end '...I could tell this to.'

Finally, good dialogue multitasks. As Eric Bentley writes:

> An Ibsenite sentence often performs four or five functions at once. It sheds light on the character speaking, on the character spoken to, on the character spoken about; it furthers the plot; it functions ironically in conveying to the audience a meaning different from that conveyed to the characters.[5]

Time devices

Clocks

Theatre is a two-sense medium (sight and hearing) and therefore a two-dimension medium (operating in both space and time). There are moments when the event is only operating on one plane (though rarely: a silence is all about time, and a scene set in the dark isn't radio). But both have to be present and if they aren't, you don't have a play.

I want first to deal with devices largely about time, including a raft of devices concerned with theatrical rhythm (**tempo**) and a menu of devices collectively called **figuring**. First, I want to talk about the most obvious element of time in the theatre, which is the use of **clocks**.

The American legal-thriller writer John Grisham's sixth rule for writing successful thrillers is: 'Give the protagonist a short time limit, then shorten it.'[6] Gore Vidal put it another way: when Jay Parini asked him, 'Do you think I can have characters talking for fourteen or fifteen pages about history, aesthetics and such things?', Vidal replied: 'Only if they are sitting in a railway carriage and there is bomb under the seat.'[7] It's a kind of miracle how time pressure can intensify a scene, even if the pressurising factor is peripheral to its course. In the first scene of my play *Pentecost*, an East European museum curator explains to a British art historian how she discovered a hitherto-unknown and possibly very valuable fresco behind layers of whitewash, plaster and brick on the wall of an abandoned church. To intensify a dense, expositional scene, I imagined that the art historian had been on his way to speak at a formal dinner, and the curator had (effectively) kidnapped him, driving him some distance into the countryside to look at the fresco, as the minutes ticked by. What I'd done was to follow Gore Vidal's advice: I'd put a clock on the scene.

The most obvious clock is the task that has to be completed before something catastrophic happens (in the silent movie, the heroine must be detached from the rails before the 4.05 passes over her). But there are many variations. Sometimes – as in the 4.05 train or countless countdowns to explosions or executions – we know how long we've got. Other times, we know something or someone is coming or going – like Morton in *The Winslow Boy* – but we don't quite know when. In the last scene of *Romeo and Juliet*, as Paris challenges Romeo outside the Capulet tomb, Paris's page announces that he's going to call the watch; from then on, the clock is ticking, just as it starts ticking as soon as a character telephones for a taxi in David Hare's *Skylight*. In the Porter scene in *Macbeth* we hear the clock, which takes the form of an increasingly urgent knocking on the castle door. In Jean Anouilh's *Poor Bitos*, David Hare's *Plenty* and Charlotte Keatley's *My Mother Said I Never Should*, conversations are given impetus and urgency by car horns blaring outside. From very early on in the last act of *The Cherry Orchard*, characters insist that unless they leave now 'we'll miss the train'; in Noël Coward's *Still Life* (a love story set in a railway station) the clock of the characters' arriving and departing trains propels or frustrates the action. Polonius's farewell speech of advice to his son is given added impetus – and comic force – by the fact that we know Laertes' ship is waiting: his twenty-six-line speech begins: 'Yet here, Laertes? Aboard, aboard, for shame!' There are scenes in which the deadline is passed: in the trial scene in Brecht's *Galileo*, the hour at which Galileo's recantation is to be marked by the tolling of a bell passes in silence (to the joy of Galileo's assistants), only for the bell to toll a minute or so later. There are scenes in which the action is simply hurried along: as when Northumberland taps his watch – as it were – to separate King Richard and Queen Isabella towards the end of *Richard II* ('Take leave and part, for you must part forthwith'), as indeed Catesby asks Hastings to hurry up his doomladen prophecy in *Richard III* ('come come, dispatch') on the grounds that the Duke of Gloucester would like to see Hastings's head detached from his body before dinner.

In addition to different kinds of clock (some shortening deadlines, some lengthening them), there are double clocks: in the tavern scene in *Henry IV, Part One*, Poins's insistent calling for the drawer Francis is a little clock, and the expected arrival of the police is the big one, again lengthened rather than shortened in the scene (the action is twice interrupted by what we might think to be the authorities but which turns out to be somebody else). In Act 2 of *Three Sisters*, we are reminded of the big clock (the coming of the carnival revellers to the house, shortly after nine) by the ticking of the small clock (Vershinin's insistent demands for tea).

While on no less than three occasions in *Romeo and Juliet* the Nurse delays imparting vital information to junior or senior Capulets (about Romeo's plans for an assignation, Romeo's banishment and Juliet's 'death'). Like *Waiting for Godot*, the last act of Arnold Wesker's *Roots* is all about waiting for an off-stage character to arrive (in this case, the protagonist Beattie Bryant's Communist boyfriend Ronnie, for whom Beattie's Norfolk family have prepared a huge spread, reminding us of his anticipated arrival throughout the action). In my version of *Dr Jekyll and Mr Hyde* I employed the old chiller trick of building up to a horror moment – the first appearance of Hyde – and then puncturing the expectation by bringing on an untransformed Jekyll, in order to increase the shock of Hyde's actual entrance a page or two later (as the shock of Galileo's recantation is increased by the false relief of the deadline passing). Following the sound of an offstage shot, the climax of Ibsen's *The Wild Duck* turns into a game of Cluedo, with the company not only searching every room but speculating as to every possible perpetrator – and victim – before the awful truth is realised and the child Hedvig's body carried on to the stage (and even now, as with Lear over Cordelia, we are faced with the agony of Hjalmar's refusal to accept that Hedvig is dead).

In Willy Russell's one-woman *Shirley Valentine*, a middle-aged housewife's life is transformed by a holiday; asked why the first act sustains so well, Russell answers simply: 'The time bomb of Greece.' There's another time bomb in the first act of Prichard's *Essex Girls*, in which three schoolgirls are waiting to use the toilet in a school lavatory in which one cubicle is unusable and the other is engaged, and remains so for the whole of the first act. Prichard's refusal to fulfil our expectation that we will be told who is in the locked toilet and why – though fully aware that we're waiting for that moment virtually from the word go – is an excellent example of Chekhov's law that you can only leave the gun hanging on the wall if you know that we know that that's exactly what you're doing.

Finally, there is one of the great clock scenes of drama, the screen scene in Sheridan's *The School for Scandal*. The supposedly virtuous Joseph Surface has brought the young and beautiful Lady Teazle into his first-floor drawing room in order to seduce her. Faced with a series of highly inopportune visitors (including Lady Teazle's husband), Joseph has hidden her behind a screen from both his brother Charles (who doesn't know anyone's there) and Sir Peter Teazle himself (who does, but not that it's his wife). The tension of the scene is upped by the small clock of Lady Sneerwell's arrival downstairs, to whom Joseph is forced to go in order to keep her there, but the main clock, of course, is our conventional expectation that sooner or later the screen will fall. This is what happens:

SIR PETER. Hark'ee, have you a mind to have a good laugh at Joseph?

CHARLES. I should like it of all things.

SIR PETER. Then, i'faith, we will! (*Aside.*) I'll be quit with him for discovering me. (*Whispers.*) He had a girl with him when I called.

CHARLES. What! Joseph? you jest.

SIR PETER. Hush! – a little French milliner – and the best of the jest is – she's in the room now.

CHARLES. The devil she is!

SIR PETER. Hush! I tell you. (*Points to the screen.*)

CHARLES. Behind the screen! Odds life, let's unveil her!

SIR PETER. No, no, he's coming: you shan't, indeed!

CHARLES. Oh, egad, we'll have a peep at the little milliner!

SIR PETER. Not for the world! – Joseph will never forgive me.

CHARLES. I'll stand by you –

SIR PETER. Odds, here he is!

> CHARLES SURFACE *throws down the screen. Re-enter* JOSEPH SURFACE.

CHARLES. Lady Teazle, by all that's wonderful!

SIR PETER. Lady Teazle, by all that's damnable!

CHARLES. Sir Peter, this is one of the smartest French milliners I ever saw. Egad, you seem all to have been diverting yourselves here at hide and seek, and I don't see who is out of the secret. Shall I beg your ladyship to inform me? Not a word! – Brother, will you be pleased to explain this matter? What! Morality dumb too? – Sir Peter, though I found you in the dark, perhaps you are not so now! All mute! Well – though I can make nothing of the affair, I suppose you perfectly understand one another; so I'll leave you to yourselves. (*Going.*)

Brother, I'm sorry to find you have given that worthy man grounds for so much uneasiness. – Sir Peter! There's nothing in the world so noble as a man of sentiment! (*Exit.*)

JOSEPH. Sir Peter – notwithstanding – I confess – that appearances are against me – if you will afford me your patience – I make no doubt – but I shall explain everything to your satisfaction.

SIR PETER. If you please, sir.

JOSEPH. The fact is, sir, that Lady Teazle, knowing my pretensions to your ward Maria – I say, sir, Lady Teazle, being apprehensive of the jealousy of your temper – and knowing my friendship to the family – she, sir, I say – called here – in order that – I might explain these pretensions – but on your coming – being apprehensive – as I said – of your jealousy – she withdrew – and this, you may depend on it, is the whole truth of the matter.

SIR PETER. A very clear account, upon my word; and I dare swear the lady will vouch for every article of it.

LADY TEAZLE. For not one word of it, Sir Peter!

SIR PETER. How! don't you think it worthwhile to agree in the lie?

LADY TEAZLE. There is not one syllable of truth in what that gentleman has told you.

SIR PETER. I believe you, upon my soul, ma'am!

JOSEPH (*aside to* LADY TEAZLE). 'Sdeath, madam, will you betray me?

LADY TEAZLE. Good Mr Hypocrite, by your leave, I'll speak for myself.

Tempo: drop lines, rhythm, repetition

I quote the screen scene at length because seeing it on the page demonstrates its use of the second major time device at the playwright's disposal, which is **tempo**. The rhythm of the sequence we've just read is shaped around the awaited and delayed interventions of the two people who are exposed in the scene: Joseph Surface and Lady Teazle.

It begins with a series of short lines, alternating between Sir Peter and Charles, speeding up to the climax of the flinging down of the screen. Then there is an antiphonal couplet: a line that is repeated with one word changed ('Lady Teazle, by all that's wonderful/damnable!'). At this point, we might expect (and we certainly want) to hear from the two people who are exposed by the discovery. In fact, tantalisingly, we get a long aria directed by the only wholly innocent character (Charles) alternately to two of the three other characters onstage, whereupon he goes out, leaving an ominous silence behind him. Then, finally, Joseph embarks on two, broken-lined speeches, in which he tries to come up with a plausible explanation of Lady Teazle's presence, prompted halfway through by Sir Peter (his 'If you please, sir' being a good example of a dramatically eloquent prompting line, which gives Joseph a breather but confirms that he's still on the hook). Then, finally, there comes a line from the person who has been silent thus far, Lady Teazle, whose simple statement reverses the direction of the scene.

I want to look in detail at three of the most frequently used elements of that menu. The first is the **drop line**, the technique whereby a long, often repetitive or bombastic speech is punctured by a simple, contrasting line. In this case, it's Lady Teazle's 'For not one word of it, Sir Peter.' After Jaq's speech in Caryl Churchill's *Icecream* (quoted on p. 133), Jaq's profusion of previous employment is both punctured and underlined by Vera, the other character, who responds: 'You make me feel so boring' (punctured because of its contrast to the length of the previous speech, underlined because Vera is echoing what the audience is thinking). By contrast, in *The Comedy of Errors*, Shakespeare caps a vast, thirty-seven-line speech by the aggrieved Adriana to the man she believes to be her husband (though in fact is his twin brother) with a line which is a complete surprise, at least to Adriana:

> ANTIPHOLUS OF SYRACUSE. Plead you to *me*, fair dame? I
> know you not.
> In Ephesus I am but two hours old.

Similarly, in Harold Pinter's *No Man's Land*, the longest speech in the play, Spooner's request to be taken on as Hirst's secretary, is punctured by Hirst's 'Let us change the subject.' In the tavern scene of *Henry IV, Part One*, Hal's response to Falstaff's grandiloquent plea against banishment ('I do. I will.') is made potent by its music as well as its meaning. In the last scene of *My Night with Reg*, Eric burbles on about pretty much all the other characters in the play (including offstage ones), ending up with this commentary on the dead Guy:

Can't believe it, can you? It just doesn't make sense. I
mean, it's not as if he put it around a lot. He didn't seem
to, anyway. Mind you, I suppose I didn't know him that
well.

To which John, with whom Guy was in love, responds: 'Neither
did I.'

The drop line relies on contrast: the speech or build-up is a
little longer than you'd expect in real life; the reverse a bit
quicker and crisper. Unlike direct speech in novels, stage
dialogue thrives on divergence. It's interesting that one of the
two most important, recent developments in stage-play
notation expands time and the other compresses it. Slowing
down the dialogue, the Pinter pause calls attention to what was
said before the pause and what will be said after it; it also
dramatises the isolation of Pinter's characters (the drop line
after Spooner's speech in *No Man's Land* follows a pause). By
contrast, Caryl Churchill's slash and asterisk notation for
interruptions and overlaps speeds up the dialogue by
compressing it: the slash indicates a point of interruption, the
asterisk indicates a common starting point between two
speeches. (Incidentally, Alan Ayckbourn argues that both parts
of a simultaneous dialogue can be understood by the audience,
so long as they're delivered at different speeds.)

If the pause is about melody, then the overlap is about
harmony. A fine example of **rhythm** in comic dialogue is the
opening of Act 2 of Howard Brenton's *Epsom Downs*. A Derby
runner is being led around the parade ring by a Stable Lad:

HORSE. I am a Derby outside chance.

They parade.

The mentality of a racehorse can be compared to the
mentality of a bird. Nervous, quick, shy and rather
stupid.

The HORSE *flashes his teeth at the spectators. The*
STABLE LAD *restrains him.*

STABLE LAD. Don't give me a bad time.

HORSE. Many a racehorse has a fixed idea. Chewing
blankets. Kicking buckets over. Biting blacksmiths.

They parade.

My fixed idea is that I must have a goat tied up with me, in my box. And there, tied to a stick in the Yard, when I come back from the gallops. I will kick the place down, if I don't have my goat.

They parade.

Where is my goat?

They parade.

I want my goat!

STABLE LAD. Stop thinking about your bloody goat!

The last lines are structured rhythmically, like a joke. All end with the word 'goat' (and therefore rhyme); the second and third lines also scan ('Where is my goat?', 'I want my goat!'). The last line is both predictable (it ends with the same word), and, of course, a surprise (the Stable Lad knows what the Horse is thinking).

Repetition is also crucial to the rhythm of this passage from John Godber's four-hander *Bouncers*, in which the checklist format gives the repetition a ritualistic feel:

RALPH. Time for another quick check.

They all stand in a row and check the various parts of their bodies.

LUCKY ERIC. Hair?

LES. Check.

JUDD. Tie?

LES. Check.

LUCKY ERIC. Aftershave? Cliff Richard uses this.

ALL (*sing*). 'Got myself a sleeping, walking...'

RALPH. Check.

LUCKY ERIC. Talc on genitals?

LES. Check.

LUCKY ERIC. Clean underpants?

RALPH. Well...

LES. They'll do.

LUCKY ERIC. Money?

JUDD. Double check.

LES. Condoms?

LUCKY ERIC. Checkaroonie.

JUDD. Breath?

They all breathe out and try to smell their own breath.

ALL. Ugh!

Finally, an example of Shakespearian repetition, to demonstrate how shamelessly this essentially lyrical device can be used in prose. In *Hamlet*, there is a five-line exchange between Hamlet and Polonius about acting, in which there's one 'actor', two 'enacts', two 'killeds' and a 'kill', and puns on 'brute' and 'capital':

HAMLET. My lord, you played once i' th' university, you say.

POLONIUS. That I did, my lord, and was accounted a good actor.

HAMLET. And what did you enact?

POLONIUS. I did enact Julius Caesar. I was killed i' th' Capitol. Brutus killed me.

HAMLET. It was a brute part of him to kill so capital a calf there. Be the players ready?

By a sudden switch both of subject and vocabulary, 'Be the players ready?' functions as a drop line.

Unlike the Godber, which is choral, or *The Comedy of Errors* speech, which is in verse, the *Hamlet* dialogue is formally naturalistic, and in prose. On the other hand, there is a clear element of artifice. The difference between this and what you'd hear in real life is, of course, the frequency of repetition, and the lack of redundancy (the meaningless 'ums', 'ahs', 'wells' and 'anyways'), which reveals characteristics of the dialogue which we might miss in actual speech. The dramatist is drawing attention to the way people actually speak to each other first by noting a pattern and, then, by limiting the amount of redundant material that would obscure it.

The taking-up of phrases and repeating them for rhetorical effect is a trick that Morton frequently pulls on Ronnie in the cross-examination in *The Winslow Boy*. There is another – and wonderful – example of the same thing in Churchill's *Top Girls*. Twenty-one-year-old, unemployed Shona is trying to get on the books of an upmarket employment agency and is being interviewed by Nell:

> NELL. Is this right? You are Shona?
>
> SHONA. Yeh.
>
> NELL. It says here you're twenty-nine.
>
> SHONA. Yeh.
>
> NELL. Too many late nights, me. So you've been where you are for four years, Shona, you're earning six basic and three commission. So what's the problem?
>
> SHONA. No problem.
>
> NELL. Why do you want a change?
>
> SHONA. Just a change.
>
> NELL. Change of product, change of area?
>
> SHONA. Both.
>
> NELL. But you're happy on the road?
>
> SHONA. I like driving.
>
> NELL. You're not after management status?
>
> SHONA. I would like management status.
>
> NELL. You'd be interested in titular management status but not come off the road?
>
> SHONA. I want to be on the road.

What Churchill is doing is showing a deceitful and nervous applicant trying to do what she thinks is wanted of her by repeating elements of the question in the answer. On no less than thirteen occasions through the scene, Shona repeats a word or phrase from Nell's preceding line (in the section quoted above, the repeated words/phrases are 'problem', 'change', 'management status' and 'road'). To drive the point home, at the end of this section, Shona tries to justify her claim to be twenty-nine by saying: 'We look young. Youngness runs in the family in our family', to which Nell responds by asking Shona to describe her present job, to which Shona replies, in a semantically redundant but dramatically eloquent phrase: 'My present job at present.' Shona then embarks on a long speech, in which her claim to be a white-goods saleswoman falls apart, and Nell realises she's been fed a pack of lies.

The two 'youngs', two 'familys' and three 'presents' cap the eleven previous repetitions. The audience will almost certainly notice the device (though it might be picked up subliminally). But Churchill doesn't do it in every exchange. In fact, there are twenty-nine exchanges in the scene. Let's imagine that, in real life, Shona might have repeated an element of the question in around eight or nine of the answers. Had Churchill made every answer contain a word from the question, her strategy would have been over-obvious (indeed, the scene would become a kind of lyric). Thirteen echoing exchanges is enough to draw attention to the syndrome, but not enough to seem forced or artificial.

Finally, antiphonal speaking is the basis of the Cecily/Gwendolen tea-party argument in *The Importance of Being Earnest*, reaching its climax with the contest of the diaries which leads to one of the great put-downs of dramatic literature. In a sense, *Top Girls* uses the same words to express something different (a probing questioning, a nervous response). The repetitive technique that Wilde uses is quite simply a series of antiphonal lines expressing an equivalent meaning in different words. Gwendolen and Cecily have just met, and are getting on famously, when Cecily makes a confession:

> CECILY (*rather shy and confidingly*). Dearest Gwendolen, there is no reason why I should make a secret of it to you. Our little county newspaper is sure to chronicle the fact next week. Mr Ernest Worthing and I are engaged to be married.
>
> GWENDOLEN (*quite politely, rising*). My darling Cecily, I think there must be some slight error. Mr Ernest Worthing is engaged to me. The announcement will appear in the *Morning Post* on Saturday at the latest.
>
> CECILY (*very politely, rising*). I am afraid you must be under some misconception. Ernest proposed to me exactly ten minutes ago. (*Shows diary.*)
>
> GWENDOLEN (*examines diary through her lorgnette carefully*). It is certainly very curious, for he asked me to be his wife yesterday afternoon at 5.30. If you would care to verify the incident, pray do so. (*Produces diary of her own.*) I never travel without my diary. One should always have something sensational

to read in the train. I am so sorry, dear Cecily, if it is
any disappointment to you, but I am afraid I have the
prior claim.

CECILY. It would distress me more than I can tell you,
dear Gwendolen, if it caused you any mental or
physical anguish, but I feel bound to point out that
since Ernest proposed to you he clearly has changed
his mind.

GWENDOLEN (*meditatively*). If the poor fellow has been
entrapped into any foolish promise I shall consider it
my duty to rescue him at once, and with a firm hand.

CECILY (*thoughtfully and sadly*). Whatever unfortunate
entanglement my dear boy may have got into, I will
never reproach him with it after we are married.

GWENDOLEN. Do you allude to me, Miss Cardew, as an
entanglement? You are presumptuous. On an
occasion of this kind it becomes more than a moral
duty to speak one's mind. It becomes a pleasure.

CECILY. Do you suggest, Miss Fairfax, that I entrapped
Ernest into an engagement? How dare you? This is
no time for wearing the shallow mask of manners.
When I see a spade I call it a spade.

GWENDOLEN (*satirically*). I am glad to say that I have
never seen a spade. It is obvious that our social
spheres have been widely different.

For all its brilliance, there is – out of context – something a bit
arch about the musical balance of the duologue. What makes
it sing dramatically is its coherence not just within the scene
but within the play. The argument between the two women has
been predicted (Algernon remarks in Act 1 that before women
call each other sisters they call each other a lot of other things
first, which is exactly what they proceed to do). Cecily's diary
too has been set up in her earlier scene with her governess Miss
Prism, and reiterated in her scene with the man she thinks is
Ernest Worthing (in fact, Algernon), in which she has
chronicled their burgeoning, imaginary courtship. In setting-
up, reiterating and paying-off Cecily's diary, Wilde is employing
another important device.

Figuring (1): signing

Figuring is a technique whereby we draw attention to the relationship between different elements in plays (including lines, themes, character traits, formats, plot points and devices). The two main types of figuring are analogous to biologist Steven Rose's two varieties of scientific study: 'The search for underlying regularities in seemingly dissimilar phenomena; and the analysis of the causes of variation – small differences in seemingly similar phenomena.'[8] So, in plays, **rhyming** emphasises the similarity between superficially distinct elements, while **signing** draws attention to differences between the seemingly repeated. Rhyming tends to involve pairings, while signing often works in threes: the set-up (or plant) followed by a reiteration, culminating in a pay-off (there can be a number of reiterations, and a subsequent echo). The skill of signing is, of course, to make the set-ups and reiterations memorable without revealing the fact that they are part of an architecture (or revealing their *place* in an architecture).

The most obvious way of doing this – as Wilde proves with the set-up both of the Gwendolen/Cecily argument and Cecily's diary – is to disguise the set-up as a joke in itself. One of the reasons why the sitcom *Fawlty Towers* is so effective is that almost all its plot set-ups – the fuses laid in the first half of an episode that pay-off in the second – look like free-standing jokes, giving pleasure by themselves and concealing their structural purpose. We've seen how the bombastic Captain Brazen's insistence that Judge Balance's name is Laconic is set up, reiterated and paid off in Farquhar's *The Recruiting Officer* (p. 46). Structurally, the idol which appears in all three of the timescales of Brenton's *The Romans in Britain* is a sign. There is hardly a line in Noël Coward's *Private Lives* which doesn't set something up, reiterate it, or pay it off. The most substantial sign is a rule which the divorced-but-reunited Elyot and Amanda impose on each other to prevent their arguments spiralling out of control: if one of them senses a row beginning, they'll say 'Solomon Isaacs' and a two minutes' silence will begin. This rule is invented (and meets its first test) at the end of the first act, as Elyot and Amanda abandon their new spouses (during their honeymoons) to run away to Amanda's Paris apartment together. It's reiterated, early in Act 2, in Paris, where the codeword is shortened to 'Sollox'. There are then two successful impositions of the rule (after the first cooling-off period, Elyot says, 'Near thing'; during the second, he plays the piano). Thick with coding, the third 'Sollox' fails, a fight breaks out, and the two abandoned spouses enter to interrupt it.

The provocation for the last argument is Elyot's irritation at Amanda's playing the gramophone (itself a retaliation for Elyot's brandy-drinking). He claims that the music will annoy the neighbours; Amanda insists the neighbours are in Tunis, to which Elyot responds: 'This is no time of the year for Tunis', thus establishing the North African resort as part of their conversational code. When, in the third act, Amanda wants to dramatise her guilt to her new and abandoned husband Victor, she demands that he divorce her, whereupon she'll 'go away, far away, Morocco or Tunis or somewhere', and probably die of some terrible disease. Later, when speaking more realistically about her future, she is challenged by Victor ('You said just now you were going away to Tunis, to die'), to which she responds by quoting Elyot: 'I've changed my mind, it's the wrong time of the year for Tunis.' Not surprisingly, his response is to ask her 'Why won't you be serious for just one moment?', which links the Tunis sign with the flippancy sign which also runs through the last act, culminating in the predictable argument between the two abandoned spouses at the end. Throughout *Private Lives* – and indeed throughout Coward – there are 'Solloxes' and 'Tunises', through which Coward unites and divides his characters.

'Sollox' and 'Tunis' move between acts, but it's possible for a sign to be set up, reiterated and paid off within one scene. The last scene of the first act of David Hare's *Plenty* is set during the Suez crisis of late 1956. Diplomat Raymond Brock is entertaining an official from the Burmese Embassy (M. Aung) and his wife at his house. The other main guest – Brock's superior, Leonard Darwin – has been delayed at the Foreign Office by the crisis. When he arrives, Brock's 'dangerously cheerful' wife Susan appears to be supportive (assuring Darwin that 'the words "Suez Canal" will not be spoken'), but goes on to make her own opinion of the Suez invasion abundantly clear ('nobody will say blunder or folly or fiasco. Nobody will say "international laughing stock". You are among friends'). She then takes M. Aung into another room, leaving Brock and Darwin alone.

During their ensuing conversation, Darwin tells Brock of his anguish over the British role in the Suez invasion, and Brock asks Darwin if he's going to resign. Before that, however, Darwin has asked after Mme Aung, and made the prediction that she will be culturally inclined: 'Traditional dance, she'll tell us about, in the highlands of Burma.' When the rest of the party re-enters, this prediction is fulfilled (and the sign reiterated) when Susan tells us that Mme Aung 'has been enthralling us with the story of the new Bergman film at the Everyman', and Mme Aung opines that 'the Norwegians are very good at that sort of thing'. Susan becomes increasingly aggressive, not least to her husband Brock, who tries to use the Bergman film to change the subject. Unfortunately the plot of the film turns out to be uncomfortably close to the situation in the room:

> BROCK. Will you please be quiet? (*Pause.*) The story of the film.
>
> MME AUNG. There's a woman... who despises her husband...

At this point, we're invited to think that Mme Aung's embarrassment is the pay-off of the sign which began with Darwin's prediction. But in fact Hare has concealed within the first reiteration a second set-up, which gives Darwin his exit line. After another blow-up between Brock and Susan ('Please can you stop,' begs Brock, 'can you stop fucking talking for five fucking minutes on end?'), Darwin decides to leave. Before he goes, he requests permission to set Mme Aung right on a point of fact, explaining that 'Ingmar Bergman is not a bloody Norwegian, he is a bloody Swede.' This undiplomatic language gives Brock the answer to his question: Darwin is going to resign.

This sign in *Plenty* pays off with a character behaving uncharacteristically. Another example of this occurs in Callie Khouri's film *Thelma and Louise*, in which two women embark on a road-trip without their husbands. Thelma is sexually assaulted, Louise shoots and kills the rapist, and the women become outlaws. Later, Louise has money wired to her by her partner, and Thelma picks up a personable young thief (against Louise's advice). In their motel bedroom, the young man demonstrates the entertaining patter he uses when holding-up convenience stores, to Thelma's evident delight. In the motel diner the following morning, Thelma tells Louise about her night of passion. Suddenly, Louise realises that Thelma has left their money in Thelma's room, from which, of course, the young thief has taken it. On the run and now destitute, Louise is in despair. Thelma promises to resolve the situation. She robs a convenience store, using the same patter that her unreliable lover taught her.

The sequence feels like a fairy tale (the use of a weapon, unexpectedly gained, in order to redress the ill done by its provider). So it should: the superficially useless weapon provided by the donor in the Proppian folktale is an excellent example of a sign: something set up in one context, and reappearing in another. The second act of Mamet's *Oleanna* is built round the student's rereading of the lecturer's attempts to make her feel better in Act 1 ('He told me that if I would stay alone with him in his office, he would change my grade to an A.')

It will be clear from all these examples that we are talking about encoding, and the accretion of layers and layers of new meaning to elements and images, each time they appear (in *Plenty*, the Bergman film is never just a Bergman film). In John Osborne's *The Entertainer*, the washed-up comedian Archie Rice has a speech about a blues singer he once heard in America:

> *Now you're going to smile at this*, you're going to smile your educated English head off, because I suppose you've never sat lonely and half-slewed in some bar among strangers a thousand miles from anything you think you understand. But if ever I saw any hope or strength in the human race, it was in the face of that old fat negress getting up to sing about Jesus or something like that.

Later he connects the woman's singing with his own failure:

> There's nobody who can feel like that. I wish to God I could, I wish to God I could feel like that old black bitch with her fat cheeks, and sing. If I'd done one thing as good as that in my whole life, I'd have been all right.

Having encoded the woman as an emblem of the pure emotion that Archie realises he's never been able to express, the scene moves on. At the end of it, news comes that Archie's son Mick – kidnapped while serving in the British Army at Suez – has been killed. Archie's response is to evoke the woman he heard in the bar, by singing a line from her blues.

Such encoding can reveal major plot developments. In *The Madness of George III*, Alan Bennett encodes the phrase 'what what?' as the king's (irritating) mannerism, and reiterates it when the servants note that, once mad, he doesn't use it any more. The phrase is thus encoded as an index of his mental health and, when we hear it again, we know he's regained it. Similarly in my play about a schizophrenic woman in the 1960s, *Mary Barnes*, the protagonist's psychiatrist sets up a running trope, asking Mary, 'Knock knock. Who's there? Mary. Mary who?', a game which Mary plays but refuses to finish. So once again the refusal to say her own surname is encoded for use at the play's climax.

In both *George III* and *Mary Barnes*, the audience has laughed at the set-up; they laugh again at the pay-off, but the laughter is now invested with the emotion of the trope's encoded meaning. It seems near to a rule: if you want to make audiences cry, make them laugh at the same thing first.

So, in the tavern scene in *Henry IV, Part One*, we enjoy Falstaff's bombastic pleas to the same degree as we're moved by the prince's rejection. In *Romeo and Juliet*, the fact that we have laughed at the Nurse's refusal to tell Juliet what she so desperately wants to hear (the outcome of the Nurse's meeting with Romeo) intensifies the pathos of the scene in which the Nurse has to tell Juliet what she doesn't want to hear (that Romeo is banished). In my adaptation of *Nicholas Nickleby*, I used – as it happens – a scene from *Romeo and Juliet* to similar effect. Nicholas and Smike – the crippled orphan child he has rescued from a brutal Yorkshire school – are taken up by a travelling theatre company, the standard of which can be judged from the fact that three weeks after joining, Nicholas is playing Romeo. Smike is playing the Apothecary in the Mantua scene, and there is a comic sequence in which Nicholas teaches Smike his lines, particularly the Apothecary's opening cry: 'Who calls so loud?' The actual performance of the beginning of the scene, seen from the wings, is also a moment of comedy, and later on in the play the words of this scene – the high point of Smike's young life – become a kind of code between the two friends, used to refer comically to their experiences in the world. However, when Smike is dying, the words return again, this time in a tragic context, as Smike uses Romeo's words about Juliet to describe his own doomed love for Nicholas's sister, and dies, looking upwards, with the cry: 'Who calls? Who calls so loud?'

Similarly, in the film *E.T.*, screenwriter Melissa Mathison encodes the fact that the Extra-Terrestial and the boy Elliot relate telepathically through comedy. Set up in the scene when ET gets accidentally drunk and Elliot – unknowingly drunk in psychic sympathy – releases frogs in his classroom, the figure is reiterated when ET watches a screen kiss and Elliot kisses a girl at school. Establishing the relationship comically intensifies the emotion when Elliot and ET are both dying. Similarly, ET's power of healing is set up as part of the process of ET learning to talk, with the word 'Ouch', a sign reiterated (again comically) when ET tries to 'cure' what in fact is a joke Hallowe'en costume wound in front of Elliot's mother, threatening his 'disguise'. Once again, when ET and Elliot share the pain of their parting with the word 'Ouch' at the end, the moment is made more powerful, as well as less sentimental, than it would be, had it not been planted in a different way.

I've touched on my final example already. In the last chapter (p. 137-8), I referred to the scene in Brian Friel's *Translations* in which it's established that the Gaelic of the County Donegal villagers and the English of the British Army are both rendered in English, and that the purpose of the British Army's presence is to map the county, and to substitute Anglicised, 'rational' place names for those in the original Gaelic.

Subsequently, British Army Lieutenant Yolland demonstrates his increasing sympathy with the villagers by trying to learn the original place names that his superiors have charged him to change, and we become aware that part of this sympathy is specifically directed to Maire, who gives him permission to attend the village dance. Earlier in the play we have learnt that Maire speaks some basic words of English ('earth', 'fire') and one strange sentence she has picked up in her youth: 'In Norfolk we besport ourselves around the maypole.'

On the night of the dance, Yolland and Maire leave the party and run outside. Friel then rings almost every conceivable change on two people trying to communicate in what is for us the same language but for them is mutually incomprehensible. They express what are (unbenownst to them) the same ideas in dissimilar and then similar words: 'The grass must be wet. My feet are soaking'; 'Your feet must be wet. The grass is soaking.' Maire tries Latin – in Latin – but Yolland doesn't have it. Inspired by his recognising her pronunciation of his name, Maire lists her basic English words, which she then 'translates' into Irish to teach him. Then she tries her maypole sentence, which Yolland misunderstands, and she fears she's learnt something dirty. Then Yolland lists the old Gaelic place names; as they both know them they can speak them antiphonally. They speak again across each other, but now conscious that their meaning is the same. Finally, Yolland uses the word 'always' – in English – which Maire picks up as significant and asks about, but Yolland cannot understand. A few lines later, Maire uses the Gaelic for 'always' which Yolland picks up as significant and asks about but she can't understand ('"Always?" What is that word – "always"?'). And then they kiss.

This sequence contains almost everything I've spoken of about scenes. It has a clear action: 'Despite not sharing a language, two young people succeed in communicating their love for each other.' It has a format – teaching and translating – with a number of constituent protocols to do with testing and exploration, and a number of consequent devices, including antiphonal speech and repetition. It is full of reiterations, echoes and pay-offs of lines and devices that we have earlier laughed at and which now move us. It is also another kind of figure. Almost everything about the previous translation scene is different from this one. But by echoing its format, Friel draws attention to what the two scenes have in common.

Figuring (2): rhyming

If signing invites us to contrast, to note dissimilar uses of the same thing (the Bergman film is, in *Plenty*, a character point for Mme Aung, a mechanism for demonstrating how badly

Susan is behaving, and a means of revealing Darwin's decision to resign), then **rhyming** invites us to compare things that on the surface look distinct. The most striking examples are biblical: the miracle of Pentecost rhyming with the Tower of Babel; the turning of the water into wine at Cana prefiguring the turning of wine into blood at the Last Supper; the spices brought by three wise men to Christ's birthplace foreshadowing those brought by the three Marys to his tomb.

In Shakespeare, rhyming is the mechanism by which the mirroring of plots and subplots is initially concealed from the audience. The two plots of *The Merchant of Venice* seem sharply distinct: the one among merchants and moneylenders in the city, the other in the green world of Portia's country mansion. They are linked by the character of Bassanio, who needs money from Antonio to fund his bid for Portia's hand, but, just as importantly, by an unjust law: the Venetian 'pound of flesh' penalty for bad debts and Portia's father's ruling that his daughter shall marry the winner of a 'take your pick' contest between the contents of a gold, silver and lead casket. Both Antonio (in borrowing from Shylock, which may lead to his death) and Bassanio (in entering a contest which, if he loses it, will require him to commit to a lifetime's celibacy) make high-risk promises. We are invited to note these comparisons by an unexpected echo between the first lines of each plot: Antonio starts the play with the line: 'In sooth, I know not why I am so sad'; Portia's first words are: 'By my troth, Nerissa, my little body is aweary of this great world.'

Similarly, the connection between Falstaff's presumed death on the battlefield at Shrewsbury (at the end of *Henry IV, Part One*) and the presumed death of King Henry (towards the end of *Henry IV, Part Two*) is underlined by the fact that it's Prince Henry – in both cases – who does the presuming. This situational rhyme supports a bigger, structural rhyme between the Part One tavern scene (which consists of two big, set-piece confrontations interrupted by an interlude) and the Part Two death scene, in which the prince speaks to what he believes is his father's corpse, leaves, and is summoned back to conduct the obligatory deathbed conversation. The final connection is metonymic: in the tavern scene play-acting, both Falstaff and Hal use a cushion for the crown; in the death scene, the prince takes the crown from the 'dead' king, puts it on and has to give it back.

Sometimes a situation is encoded in one way and repeated in a way which invites us to assume that the earlier coding is still operative. An example is the section of the first act of Ibsen's *Rosmersholm*, during which Johannes Rosmer's helpmeet Rebecca West is trying to persuade Rosmer to admit to the orthodox and conservative headmaster Kroll that he (Rosmer) has lost his religious faith. Into this unresolved dilemma comes Rosmer's old mentor, the semi-dissolute Brendel, who although a failure still has enough spark to prod and provoke Kroll. Impressed that Brendel has retained the courage to live his life his own way, and following both Brendel and Rebecca's exits, Rosmer confesses his apostasy. Technically, Brendel's little scene has raised the tension of Rosmer's decision by delaying it. But although unmentioned, the scene has clearly had the effect of changing Rosmer's mind, and Brendel is thus encoded as a provoker of such changes. So when in Act 4, Rosmer and Rebecca face a life-and-death decision together, and Brendel appears for a second time, we are invited to assume that what he says will make up their minds for them, which indeed it does. Though in this case, it operates in reverse: it is Brendel's loss of ideals during his absence from the stage that inspires Rosmer to follow his ideals – wisely or not – into the river and beyond the grave.

Structuring whole plots in Shakespeare, focusing on key turning points in Ibsen, rhyming can also work much more elliptically. In the first act of Rebecca Prichard's *Essex Girls* (three girls in a school toilet) we are waiting for a fourth girl to appear from the only usable lavatory (which she never does). In Act 2 (two young women in a high-rise flat), a mother ignores the cries of her baby through the intercom from the next room. As the absent baby clearly rhymes with the non-emergent fourth girl, we are led to assume that the baby too will remain offstage. So when the mother's friend goes out to the baby, calms her, and brings her on, the structure is inviting us to see this as a discreet message of hope.

Soliloquies and speeches

The first act of *Essex Girls* consists of punchy, racket-shot dialogue; the second act opens with what is effectively a single long speech by one character, punctuated by the odd phatic 'yeah' and 'nah' by the other. If consequential dialogue is a high virtue in contemporary drama, then great speeches tend to be looked down on as vessels for that 'empty rhetoric' which is, for Eric Bentley, the original sin of classical dramatic writing. In a round defence of musicals, the director Neil Bartlett correctly points out that no one ever turned to their lover and whispered, 'Darling, they're saying our speech.'

Chekhov swore that he'd eliminate one form of great speech, the soliloquy, entirely from his work, dramatising the characters' inner lives through subtext and inference. There is a small cheat in *Three Sisters*, when Andrei opens his heart to the deaf Ferapont ('If you *could* hear, I doubt if I'd be talking to you like this'), and a larger one at the end of *The Cherry Orchard*, when the old servant Firs, alone and abandoned in the locked-up house, mutters a dying speech. But, generally, Chekhov succeeded in his ambition. In the same way, the aside, spoken exclusively to the audience during a peopled scene, is particularly associated with Restoration drama, and is thought to have died with the end of that golden period.

In fact, the aside is one of the many rhetorical devices which British playwrights reminted during the general freeing-up of naturalistic convention in the 1970s. Salieri is constantly throwing lines to the audience in Peter Shaffer's *Amadeus*; Brenton's *Epsom Downs* has lots of asides, including, in its way, those made by the Horse. Along with asides, the soliloquy has returned to fashion: David Hare's 2008 *Gethsemane* gives between-scene soliloquies to six of the play's nine characters. The sense, in most of them, of the characters speaking in knowing confidence to people largely but not entirely like them ('You may be surprised by some of this,' they appear to be saying, 'but you'll understand the point') underlines the fact that *Gethsemane*'s out-front speeches represent a time and space jump; it drags the past tense of the play into the present tense of the performance, and the site of the play from the stage to the whole theatre. A stage soliloquy is seldom a contemplation, much more often a performance; debating to whom the Duke of Gloucester was speaking in his opening soliloquies, director Bill Alexander suggested to actor Antony Sher that the usurper was neither writing a confession nor drafting his defence, but conducting a seminar: his audience was a convention of trainee Richard IIIs.[9]

The place of the long speech delivered to others is as striking a feature of post-war British drama as is the revival of the aside and the soliloquy. Following Darwin's abrupt exit, Susan closes Act 1 of *Plenty* with a speech which starts out as something like a poem ('Isn't this an exciting week? Don't you think? Isn't this thrilling? Don't you think?') and ends by explaining the title: 'There is plenty. Shall we eat again?' Set in London in May 1968, the first act of Trevor Griffiths's *The Party* is built round two huge socialist polemics to which the other characters have gathered to listen. Scene 7 of Sarah Daniels' *Masterpieces* consists entirely of Hilary's description of an attempt to use Coca-Cola as a contraceptive, and is one of the funniest scenes written in English in my lifetime. Harold Pinter's transformation of dramatic dialogue has blinded some critics to the power (and humour) of his long speeches: examples include Lenny's anecdote about moving an iron mangle in *The Homecoming* (drop line: 'Excuse me, shall I take this ashtray out of your way?'), Duff's minute description of the barrelling of beer in *Landscape*, and Briggs's equally detailed warning against entering the one-way system around Bolsover Street in *No Man's Land*. And *The Caretaker* contains examples of two usages of the long speech which are particularly prominent in post-war British drama.

One is the speech which ends with a dying fall. At the climax of David Hare's *The Absence of War*, the leader of the Labour Party, drilled and regimented by his helpers, breaks from his written text and opens his heart to his audience. At last, we think, he will recapture his former political passion, uncompromised by calculation. After a few sentences, however, he realises his old rhetorical skills have deserted him, and he is forced back to the speech his aides wrote for him. Such failures of nerve pepper the work of social dramatists back to and including John Osborne. Most people remember the 'no good brave causes left' speech which Jimmy Porter delivers to his friend Cliff in *Look Back in Anger*, but not that it ends bathetically, with Cliff being handed not a revolutionary placard or manifesto but a clean shirt. In fact, almost all of Jimmy's thirteen tirades end with some kind of deflating moment: either an internal non sequitur, or an inconsequential line by another character, or the realisation that the other character hasn't been listening at all. Such punctured rhetoric is the lingua franca of Simon Gray's *Butley*, Tom Stoppard's *Jumpers* and indeed playwrights of David Hare's generation and its successors. An extreme example of a speech running out of steam is the last speech of *The Caretaker*, in which the tramp Davies pleads, Falstaff-like, not to be banished from Aston's house ('Would you... would you let... would you... if I got down... and got my...').

At the end of the second act of *The Caretaker* there is another kind of speech, in which Aston tells Davies about his history of mental illness, and particularly about his electro-convulsive therapy. Clearly, Aston has never told anyone this before, and the speech ends positively (and movingly), when Aston commits himself to building a shed in the garden. Aston's speech is an example of the other notable form of long speech in post-war British theatre, in which a person – most usually a woman – finds their own articulacy and successfully expresses it. This is what happens when the working-class Beattie Bryant, realising that her charismatic boyfriend Ronnie has stood her up, finds her own voice at the end of Arnold Wesker's *Roots*; an epiphany directly echoed in Trevor Griffiths's *Comedians*, Willy Russell's *Educating Rita* and Jim Cartwright's *Road* ('Anyway I never spoke such speech in my life,' says Louise, 'and I'm glad I have').

These two devices – the dying fall and the epiphany – express the contest that dominates the political dramas of the post-war period. The descent from bang into whimper dramatises the failure of honest conviction to overcome the hypocrisy and cynicism of post-war life. When a hitherto silent person finds their voice, they confirm our faith in the possibility of political and social emancipation. Gouge out the speeches from post-war British drama, and you'd erase the meaning as definitively as if you cut all the speeches from Shakespeare.

Space devices

Location and props

Where a play or scene is set, how that setting relates to its implied location and the changing configuration of characters onstage are among the choices which enable devices based on **space**, on what the audience sees. The fact that drama can operate in time but not space (on the radio), but not in space without time is an index of the greater consequence of time devices. But the playwright who pays no attention to space is writing in the dark.

As we've established, the first decision a playwright makes about a scene is its **location**. In many scenes, they have little choice: the court scene in the throne room, the war scene on the battlefield. But, as it's sometimes effective to set scenes in unlikely locations (sex in the office, meals in bed), an unexpected location can enable events to be shown from an intriguing angle. Shakespeare often presents great events from the sidelines. In *Troilus and Cressida*, the return of the Trojan Army from battle is seen from Pandarus and Cressida's point of view, watching from above (the format is a kind of running commentary or indeed a roll-call). In both *The Winters' Tale* and *Henry VIII*, great events at court are related as gossip by citizens meeting conveniently in the street. In *Richard II*, Queen Isabella learns of her husband's abdication by overhearing a conversation between two gardeners. Similarly, the first scene of Ibsen's *The Wild Duck* is a discussion between servants in the drawing room next to the dining room from which the main characters are to appear. The whole of Stoppard's *Rosencrantz and Guildenstern are Dead* is about seeing familiar events – the story of *Hamlet* – from an unfamiliar angle.

The nature of the setting can imply what surrounds it. The love scene in *Translations* is the only scene in the play set out of doors, and begins by establishing its physical relationship to an offstage scene (the party in the village hall). Edward Bond is also expert in setting the scene within a spacial configuration: we are always made aware of the next-door room, the nearby village, the opposite bank of the river. In this, as in other matters, Bond follows Brecht, whose scenes almost always tell us about the offstage environment, and whose decisions about setting enable the action. Twice in *Galileo* we await great decisions in adjacent places: first, in the Hall of the Collegium Romanum in Rome, as the Papal Astronomer Clavius deliberates over Galileo's findings (his conclusion is delivered, offhand, as he strides across the stage, to the last monk in the line: 'He's right'). Later, in the Florentine Embassy, Galileo's team waits for the outcome of his trial. While in the penultimate scene of *Mother Courage*, the dumb Kattrin climbs on an onstage roof to bang a drum, warning an offstage town in the valley below of an imminent attack.

A particularly effective choice of setting within a location was made by David Eldridge in his early play *Falling*. A nervous newcomer is introduced into a family, and Eldridge decided to dramatise the consequent tensions by having the newcomer spill red wine onto a white carpet. The brilliant decision was to place the scene, not in the living room with the carpet, but in the kitchen, into which all the characters hurry to gather up the equipment related to their particular theory about how to avoid a permanent stain. The drying stain itself provides a most effective clock, as the characters speed about the kitchen, enabling Eldridge to reveal character as well as dramatise his action.

The spilled wine is what Brecht calls a *Gestus*, an emblem around and through which the action of the scene unfolds. Again in *Galileo*, there's a scene in which Galileo wants to demonstrate his theories of the movements of the moons of Jupiter to the boy Grand Duke of Florence, Cosimo de Medici. He fails to persuade Cosimo or his expert courtiers to look through the telescope which stands in the middle of the room. Each time Galileo pleads for them just to look through the tube, the physical object of the telescope takes on additional dramatic weight. By not being looked through, it ends up expressing the action of the scene.

Part of the power of the telescope scene is provided by our having seen the prop before: Galileo pretends to invent it in Scene 1, presents it to the Venetian Doge in Scene 2, and looks through it himself in Scene 3. Like a line, a character trait or a format, a prop can be figured. Charlotte Keatley's *My Mother Said I Never Should* covers over sixty years in the lives of four generations of women. Running through the play are various superficially banal objects that are important to the characters at various points in their lives, some of which are lost and refound: they include a doll, some flowers, a piano, painting things, a wartime utility mug, some photographs and a single red sock. Many of these objects appear in the scene in which the women are sorting through the possessions of the oldest woman (now a widow) as she prepares to leave her marital home. Having set up this language, Keatley keeps her best coup till last, when we learn that the grass-stained dress that the grandmother finds among her things was soiled on the day she lost her virginity.

The narrative of a prop can become the plot of a play. *The Coat* is an improvised play by the Serpent Players, directed by Athol Fugard. It was inspired by the story of a sixty-three-year-old ANC activist sent down for fifteen years, who handed his coat to a friend as he was led off to prison. The coat was taken back to the activist's wife, who found a lucky twist of paper in the pocket, which – for her – explained his relatively short sentence. The play arose out of speculation as to what would happen to the coat: would it be kept in tissue paper as an icon, used as a blanket in winter, or worn for a job interview? Eventually it has to be sold to keep the wife alive, so she can greet her husband when he comes back from prison.

Configuration

Both of the 'adjacent place' scenes in *Galileo* end with a crucial entrance: in the first scene, of Clavius; in the second scene, of Galileo himself. Like Joseph Surface's entrance as the screen falls in *The School for Scandal*, both of these entrances do obligatory, climactic work. But the **configuration** of characters onstage can serve many subtler functions in enabling, complicating and obstructing the advancement of action and the revelation of character. Most playwrights know the frustration of finding their characters in a configuration in which the things that need to be said can't be said, and the sense of liberation when the removal or addition of a character allows what needs to happen to occur. As Michelene Wandor points out, three characters can constitute seven different relationships, four characters 25, and five characters 121.[10]

Ibsen is brilliantly adept at using configuration to allow or to prevent things being said, in order to reveal meaning. In his late play *Little Eyolf*, a husband has recently returned from a monastic trip to the mountains. Ibsen manages to keep him and his wife onstage but never alone for most of the first act. When, finally, they are alone together, two completely different people appear before our eyes, to our surprise until we realise that Ibsen has prevented them ever having been alone in front of us before. Released from the requirement of good behaviour, the violent and bloody confrontation between these two deeply unhappy people erupts, around the issue of a book that the husband is writing and a crippled son (Little Eyolf), whose injury was caused by a moment of passionate thoughtlessness by his parents (both these matters having been discussed, with deceptive politeness, in front of the others). The husband announces that he is giving up his book (his life's work), which delights his wife, for whom the book has been an obstacle to her undiluted passion. Unfortunately, the husband goes on to explain that he's given up the book in order to devote himself entirely to bringing up his son. The wife is horrified: if he's giving up his book for anyone, it should be for her. Indeed, if the son is to be a barrier between them, she regrets having him in the first place. Both husband and wife are thus locked into Little Eyolf – for him, as a mission; for her, as a millstone – at the moment when the cry comes up from the fjord that a boy with a gammy leg is drowning.

In *Eyolf*, Ibsen assembles the right people in the right place and situation onstage for an offstage action to have its greatest impact. As Shaw describes it in his wonderful study of Ibsen ('The Quintessence of Ibsenism'[11]), he does almost precisely the opposite at the end of Act 3 of *Rosmersholm*, in which Rebecca West admits to Johannes Rosmer that she unintentionally provoked Rosmer's wife Beata into killing herself. We know that there were two reasons for this: Rebecca's ambition to force Rosmer to a higher life mission (to which Mrs Rosmer was seen as an obstacle) and her own sexual passion. But as Shaw points out, she can only confess to the ambition (not the passion) because Ibsen has placed someone else – the reactionary schoolmaster Kroll, once again – in the room with them. Further, appalled by this news, Rosmer leaves the house with Kroll, thus denying Rebecca a moment alone with him. Rebecca then calls on the housekeeper to pack, and Act 3 ends with the distinct possibility that she will leave, never seeing Rosmer again, having confessed only half of the truth.

The power of the *Rosmersholm* scene lies in a single exit which delays an obligatory revelation. If Ibsen delays obligatory moments, then Chekhov undermines and even denies them. The big news in the third act of *The Cherry Orchard* is that the family orchard has been purchased: however, this news isn't delivered by Lopakhin (the buyer) but by Anya, who reports that: 'There was somebody in the kitchen just now – he says the cherry orchard's been sold.' In the fourth act, the long-awaited scene in which we expect Lopakhin to propose to Varya is a damp squib: it ends with Lopakhin discussing the weather and Varya a broken thermometer. Meanwhile, Chekhov is preparing for his *coup de théâtre* at the end, when the old servant Firs is revealed to be locked in the empty house. He has arranged it that the only person who knows that Firs is still in the house (Varya) is offstage when Anya mistakenly reports that the old man is in the hospital.

Despite Anya's news from the kitchen, Lopakhin's entrance into the Act 3 party is a great entrance: he comes into the middle of a row between Varya and Yepikhodov (Varya nearly hits him with a stick), and he delays his announcement that he's bought the orchard until all the interested parties are assembled. Bringing people onto the stage just before the end of a scene or an act effectively throws the audience into the next one (Act 4 of *The Cherry Orchard* is entirely the consequence of what's happened in Act 3, like the fourth act of *Uncle Vanya*). It is also an example of the power of an onstage audience. Most of the talking is done by Lopakhin, but we are just as interested in the reaction of the dispossessed Madame Ranevskaya and her family.

The audience in *The Cherry Orchard* is there for a party. In Anthony Minghella's television series *What If It's Raining?* a deserted husband follows his wife into a crowded café where she's lunching with her new lover and their child. The husband's anguished pleas to his wife to return to him are given added intensity by being surrounded by other people. But the screw is given a further twist when a woman who knows the husband comes over, puts her hands over his eyes, and demands that he guess who she is. As she speaks, the husband's tears drip through her fingers. She leaves never understanding the situation she's stumbled into. The scene doesn't *need* the passer-by, but she makes it memorable. Similarly, we remember Sally's persuasive faked orgasm in *When Harry Met Sally* because she does it in a diner, everyone ends up listening, and, as she finishes, another customer tells a waiter: 'I'll have what she's having.'

It's rare to be able to compare the same scene in two configurations. In Peter Shaffer's 1979 stage play *Amadeus*, there's a scene in which the court composer Salieri composes a dull little march to mark Mozart's arrival at the court of the Emperor Joseph II. At the end of the scene all the dignitaries depart, leaving Salieri and Mozart to have a stilted conversation. Mozart compliments Salieri on 'that jolly little thing you wrote for me', sits down at the fortepiano and plays it from memory. Playing it again, he suggests that the piece could be improved ('it doesn't really *work*, that fourth – does it!') and gradually converts it into the 'Non più andrai' aria from *The Marriage of Figaro*. Mozart finishes ('with a series of triumphant flourishes and chords'), thanks Salieri once again, and leaves. Salieri turns to the audience and murmurs: 'Was it then – so early – that I began to have thoughts of murder?'

For the 1984 film version of the play (directed by Miloš Forman), Shaffer reconfigured the scene. The dignitaries remain present as Mozart accepts the Emperor's challenge to play Salieri's march from memory. They watch as Mozart plays the march, comments on its weakness ('the rest is just the same, isn't it?') and converts it into his own, celebrated melody.

Superficially, of course, the film version is more powerful: the presence of witnesses deepens Salieri's humiliation. But there are losses too. The film scene is less intense between the two men. Seeing the rest of the court responding to Mozart's insolent impetuosity takes the focus off Salieri (literally and dramaturgically), and dilutes the pressure. A scene which, in the play, is a turning point, the first major confrontation between the two protagonists, becomes, in the film, an incident in a more gradual progression.

Having configured the stage, there is a repertoire of devices to reconfigure it. We've seen how the tavern scene in *Henry IV, Part One* is built round three interruptions from outside. The screen scene in *The School for Scandal* is all about a reconfiguration. There's a great false exit in the last scene of Howard Barker's *Stripwell*, in which a released prisoner threatens the judge who sent him down with a shotgun in his home. The judge seeks to persuade the man that civilisation could not continue if prisoners sent down for six months then killed the responsible judiciary, and appears to have succeeded when the man leaves. The judge then pours himself a drink and sits, at which point the man bursts through the French windows, shouts 'No', and fires. At the end of Martin McDonagh's *The Cripple of Inishmaan*, the young woman rejects the eponymous crippled boy and walks out. There is then a whole other scene between two other characters before her head pops back in and she tells Billy:

> All right so I'll go out walking with ya, but only somewheres no fecker would see us and when it's dark and no kissing or groping, cos I don't want you ruining me fecking reputation.

The false exit works because it is – by definition – a surprise. Louise Page's 1982 play *Salonika* is set on a sandy Greek beach in the present day. An eighty-four-year-old Englishwoman, Charlotte, is sitting, looking at a sleeping, naked sunbather. Charlotte is joined by her daughter, Enid, and they talk. The expectation that the naked man will wake, stand and speak becomes almost unbearable. Finally, left alone by Enid, Charlotte tries to wake him. At that moment, someone we had no idea was there sits up out of the sand, dressed in an old-fashioned army uniform. He talks to Charlotte as if it was the most natural thing in the world. But in fact, his entrance has shifted the play back over sixty years in time, to the First World War. The someone is the ghost of Charlotte's husband.

Space in time: the ghost as the machine

The ghost's entrance in *Salonika* is a demonstration that time can operate on the plane of space. Literally embodying the past, bringing on a ghost is a dazzlingly effective way of bringing past events to life in the present and creating drama. No wonder that the ghost is one of the most consistently employed conventional devices in world theatre (far more than the aside, far more than the chorus). Its effectiveness in holding present failings and past errors to account is proved by Chairman Mao, who banned all plays with ghosts from the Chinese theatre. The earliest extant dramatic ghost is Clytemnestra in the third play of Aeschylus's *Oresteia*, *The Eumenides*. The latest has almost certainly appeared between my writing this and you reading it.

Part of the strength of ghosts is that, like formats, they bring a set of conventional expectations with them. As Mephistopheles insists in Howard Brenton's translation of Goethe's *Faust*, even devils and ghosts 'must do things by the book'. Like formats, too, those conventions can be disrupted and manipulated in order to dramatise actions. Sometimes, the ghost performs another dramatic function: in Euripides' *Hecuba*, the protagonist's drowned son Polydorus speaks the prologue. But mostly, ghosts operate with powerful but dramatically limited rules of engagement.

According to *An Index of Characters in English Printed Drama to the Restoration*[12], ghosts appear in seventy-eight pre-Commonwealth English plays (the list includes *The Jews' Tragedy*, *The Old Wives' Tale*, *The Seven Champions of Christendom*, *The Fool Would Be Favourite*, and *Grim the Collier of Croydon*). A very small number of apparitions appear in comedies: the ghost of Hercules is conjured up in Robert Greene's strange comic morality play *Friar Bacon and Friar Bungay*; a ghost is played by a puppet in Jonson's *Bartholomew Fair*. But the vast majority of ghosts appear in tragedies, in which their rules of engagement are almost always entirely clear. The ghost in Renaissance tragedy is a dead person who appears as if living to at least one living person on the stage, who instantly or eventually recognises them as a ghost and treats them as such. In many cases, such as in John Webster's *The White Devil*, the ghost of a person murdered earlier in the play appears, simply and silently, to a single lone character. In Rowley, Dekker and Ford's *The Witch of Edmonton* and Middleton's *The Changeling*, it's not clear whether silent ghosts are seen by just one person (their murderer) or by others as well.

From the beginning, the main dramatic function of ghosts is to exhort the living to exact revenge (in Tony Harrison's translation of *The Eumenides*, Clytemnesta berates the Furies: 'Dreaming not *doing*. Get up and get going. / Sleep only blunts your rage at my bloodwrong'). Although silent, Isabella's appearance to Francisco in *The White Devil* inspires him to take revenge on Bracchiano on her behalf. In Cyril Tourneur's *The Atheist's Tragedy*, the murdered Montferrers appears to his son in order to persuade him to revenge his death. In Thomas Kyd's *The Spanish Tragedy*, the ghost of Don Andrea serves, along with the character of Revenge, as the Chorus of the play. Although he witnesses events that follow his death (including the death of his murderer), Andrea does not intervene directly in the action, except as an inciter, inspirer and occasional berator of Revenge, who both predicts and promises to bring about future events, and, at the end, 'to place thy friends in ease, the rest in woes' for all eternity.

Although a much smaller part, the most dramatically active ghost in English Renaissance drama is probably Friar Comolet in George Chapman's *Bussy d'Ambois*. The Friar dies trying to prevent the Countess of Montsurry being tortured on the rack by her own husband in order to discover her liaison with Bussy d'Ambois; he returns as an umbra (or shade) to D'Ambois, as a reporter, a predictor and a director of the action. During the play he saves D'Ambois from one attempt on his life; later, when D'Ambois is dying from a pistol shot, the shade persuades him to forgive his enemies.

Shakespeare's contemporaries and successors thus developed a repertoire of conventions for the presentation of ghosts on the stage. The shade may appear silently, or speak; it may appear to one person alone on the stage or more than one; it will know the stage-present but can also, if desired, either know or predict the stage-future; it may become an active participant in the story, either by encouraging the living to take certain actions or – exceptionally – by intervening directly in the action him or herself. Consistently applied, and rational within its own terms, the ghost is in conventional terms much more like the alien or the horror monster of contemporary genres than the uncertain, unpredictable and mutating spectre of the modern ghost story.

In the four of his tragedies and one romance in which ghosts appear, Shakespeare himself employs most of these conventions (though none intervenes as directly as Friar Comolet). Eleven of Shakespeare's eighteen ghosts appear in Act 5 Scene 5 of *Richard III*, as the ghosts of Richard's victims move between his and Richmond's tents the night before the Battle of Bosworth. Although they curse Richard and bless Richmond, the ghosts do not know the outcome of the battle.

In *Julius Caesar*, the ghost of Caesar appears, again the night before the final battle, to a murderer who, unlike Richard, will fall on his own sword. Brutus is thrown by a sight that he cannot fully identify: he calls Caesar a 'monstrous apparition' and an 'ill spirit' and before Caesar disappears can do little more than echo the ghost's words:

> BRUTUS. Speak to me what thou art.
>
> GHOST. Thy evil spirit, Brutus.
>
> BRUTUS. Why com'st thou?
>
> GHOST. To tell thee thou shalt see me at Philippi.
>
> BRUTUS. Well; then I shall see thee again?
>
> GHOST. Ay, at Philippi.
>
> BRUTUS. Why, I will see thee at Philippi then.

Later, just before his death, Brutus confirms his identification of 'the ghost of Caesar', seen both before the battle and at Philippi. The ghost serves then as little more than a metaphor of Brutus's entrapment in the implications of his deed – his nemesis is Antony.

Thus far, then, Shakespeare uses his ghosts conventionally, to remind the audience of past events, to predict the future, to encourage the living to take future action and to serve as an embodiment of the conscience of those who have slain them. None of them have a central place in the plotting, and, atmospheric though they are, they could in story terms be cut. By contrast, Shakespeare's next two ghosts do something which it seems no other Renaissance playwright thought of them doing before. In both cases, they have a vital effect on the action; in the first instance initiating it, in the other provoking the move towards its catastrophe.

The ghost of Hamlet's father is Shakespeare's invention. He does not appear in Belleforest's 1570 retelling of Saxo Grammaticus's twelfth-century saga of the murder by Feng of his brother Horwendil, whose son Amleth feigns madness and succeeds in taking his revenge. This is mainly because in the original version the fratricide is no secret and thus there is no need for the ghost to reappear to tell the son what he knows already (though in Ion Caramitru's '80s Romanian *Hamlet*, rehearsed and presented in the dying years of the Ceauşescu dictatorship, the murder is common but unstated knowledge, and Hamlet is the last person in Elsinore to know). But when the ghost first appears, Horatio presumes he's come not to reveal backstory but to predict the future:

> If thou art privy to thy country's fate
> Which happily foreknowing may avoid,
> O speak!

This expectation is left to hang uncountered for two long scenes. For Shakespeare's audience the ghost's revelation in Act 1 Scene 5 would have come as a huge dramatic coup. Far from reminding the audience, and indeed the stage-present characters, of what they already know, Old Hamlet's Ghost drops the bombshell which initiates the rest of the plot. Of the plays we still have, *Hamlet* has the most active ghost both by and so far.

His later appearance – to Hamlet as he berates his mother in her chamber – marks Shakespeare's second major dramatic innovation. For the first time (again, as far as we know), a ghost appears to one of two characters onstage and is not seen by the other. 'To whom do you speak this?' she asks. 'Do you see nothing there?' he responds. 'Nothing at all,' she responds, 'yet all that is I see.'

It is this new-minted convention that Shakespeare brings to full flower in *Macbeth*, finding a devastatingly effective solution to the problem of representing a character's inner life. Macbeth's guilt at his crimes comes home to him not in private but during a state banquet (intensifying the impact by providing witnesses). Once again, Shakespeare structurally wrong-foots us. Of course, as it assembles, we ask ourselves what the banquet is *for*: but even as we put the question, Shakespeare appears to answer it with a dummy disruption, the arrival of Banquo's murderer, who whispers the news of the (partial) success of his mission to Macbeth. Lady Macbeth then spends a mere five lines summoning Macbeth back to the table before the ghost appears, unnoticed by anyone but the audience, to take Macbeth's place at table. So when, a line or two later, Macbeth expresses the cynical view that Banquo's failure to show up should be challenged for its unkindness rather than pitied for its mischance, the Jacobean playgoer will be looking forward to someone pointing out that Banquo's shade has in fact just taken his place. It is only when Lennox says 'Here is a place reserv'd' that the audience realises that Macbeth is the only one who can see him.

What follows is the dramatic representation of a man's past misdeeds returning to haunt him and an absolutely present representation of a man having a nervous breakdown. As the ghost's appearance to Hamlet but not to Gertrude is one of the moments in the play when we suspect Hamlet's sanity most strongly, so the presence of his queen and peers around Macbeth naturalises and intensifies what would, had Macbeth been alone, been a metaphor. His guests' embarrassment and his wife's panic turn an excuse for a description of Macbeth's feelings into a demonstration of a man losing control of his own suppressed emotion. And, of course, it is in the moments when Macbeth temporarily recovers his poise – dramatised by the ghost's temporary withdrawal – that we are most aware, by contrast, of the turbulent mania which Macbeth fails to suppress when the empty chair is full.

Ghosts decline in the Restoration, revive in nineteenth-century melodrama (notably, in Leopold Lewis's *The Bells*), but only appear in Ibsen in a title. Following Strindberg, they flourish across the canon.

As we've seen, Noël Coward remints the device of *The Spanish Tragedy* in his unperformed 1930 melodrama *Post-Mortem*, in which a ghost goes forward in time, from the moment of his death in the trenches to the Britain of the '30s, in which the lessons of the war are unlearnt. Anticipating Priestley's use of interwar ideas of circular time, Coward has two further intriguing ideas: one being that (by and large) the haunted persons respond in a relaxed manner to their dead son, lover, comrade and friend appearing amongst them (as Charlotte does to her husband's ghost in *Salonika*); and, second, that the ghost finds out he was wrong and his comrade in the trenches – the malevolently cynical Harry Lomas – was right about the post-war world. Disguised by some of his worst writing (and bad Coward can be very bad indeed), *Post-Mortem* has at its core a rather brilliant idea.

The rules of engagement of the ghosts in Coward's later *Blithe Spirit* are elaborate and not entirely consistent (some people see them sometimes, some people sometimes don't). But there's no question that the device of Charles Condomine's first wife reappearing to haunt his second marriage *is* the action of the play; and his positive response to the murder of his second wife by his first its message. In J.B. Priestley's *An Inspector Calls*, the policeman who exposes the role of an industrialist's family in the suicide of a young woman turns out not to exist; the arrival of (another?) Inspector at the door places the first, phantom Inspector within the tradition of the returning nemesis, speaking for a dead person to those responsible for her death.

As in so much else, post-war drama has rung infinite variations on the convention, expanding the ghost from the shade into *alter egos*, younger versions and imaginary friends. In Peter Nichols's *Passion Play*, both halves of a warring couple have *alter egos* who both contribute to and interfere with the actions of their principals. In Kay Mellor's *A Passionate Woman*, a woman's past returns in the form of a selectively visible dead lover. In Shelagh Stephenson's *The Memory of Water*, three sisters assemble for their mother's funeral, and one of them sees her mother, at the daughter's age, appearing as a ghost. In Mark Ravenhill's *Some Explicit Polaroids*, a gay ghost requests masturbation from his lover, and realises when talking to a female friend that she has no idea he's there (the only case I know of a ghost being visible to nobody onstage at all). In Alan Ayckbourn's *Invisible Friends*, the ghosts are more active: a child conjures up a perfect soulmate with whom she can secretly converse in company (when she conjures up an entire perfect alternative family things start going seriously awry). In these plays, Coward, Nichols, Mellor, Ravenhill and Ayckbourn use the targeted haunting for largely comic purposes (though Ayckbourn uses a ghost more traditionally in *Life and Beth*). In *Beside Herself*, Sarah Daniels gives her central character Evelyn an *alter ego*, Eve – unseen by any other character – whose entirely serious function is to prod Evelyn into accepting in the present what she has suppressed from her past, provoking her into remembering how she was sexually abused as a child.

Eve in *Beside Herself* is not a younger version of Evelyn, but, in Diane Samuels' play about the escape of Jewish children to Britain in the late '30s, *Kindertransport*, Evelyn is a grown-up version of a teenage refugee (called Eva in the play). Although the first act closes with the two ages of woman in brief dialogue, the doubling here is largely intended to facilitate the play's double timescale. Helen Edmundson's adaptation of *The Mill on the Floss* has three Maggie Tullivers, at different ages. In Tom Stoppard's *The Invention of Love* (which begins with a boat crossing the Styx into the Underworld) the confrontation between the younger A.E. Housman and his ghostly elder dominates the second half of Act 1, beginning with the older admitting to the younger: 'I'm not as young as I was. Whereas you of course, are.' In *Never So Good*, Howard Brenton employs the younger, First World War Harold Macmillan as a kind of conscience for the older politician. In the autobiographical *The Lady in the Van*, Alan Bennett split himself into two; confronted by this device, the Lady asks if the two Bennetts are in two minds: one says 'yes', the other says 'no'. In Michael Frayn's *Copenhagen* the three characters who speculate about what might have happened during a fifteen-minute conversation between two of them in wartime Denmark do so from the afterlife.

In these cases, splitting and ghosting serve purposes that have nothing to do with the supernatural. At the end of *Shining City*, Conor McPherson makes the ghost the central issue. Therapist Ian spends the play persuading bereaved John that his vision of his dead wife is just that. What appears to be a victory for the rational – John is finally persuaded that the ghost doesn't exist – is undermined in the play's closing seconds when, having bid goodbye to his patient, Ian closes the door, revealing the dead woman's ghost.

Many ghost plays are about people coming to terms with their own ageing. The play that treats of this subject most profoundly of all – *King Lear* – doesn't contain a ghost, but Edward Bond's 1971 reworking does. In Bond's version, Lear is befriended by a Gravedigger's Boy, whose wife, revealed in a memorable moment, is called Cordelia. The Boy is killed by Lear's daughters' soldiers, and his ghost appears to Lear in prison. In a device akin to some of the conjuration in *Macbeth*, the Boy's Ghost – who is not seen by anyone else onstage – summons Lear's daughters, as spirits, into the cell. Before Lear can be reconciled, they disappear, leaving the Boy's Ghost and Lear together. The Boy asks Lear if he can stay with him, and so he does, as a kind of supernatural conflation of the Fool and Poor Tom, for the rest of the play.

What the Boy's Ghost says to persuade Lear to keep him in his company leads me to Shakespeare's other great innovation. In most of the hauntings I've discussed, one or other of the parties is silent. In some of them, the ghost expresses fervent opinions about what is going on in the world he or she has left behind. In *Hamlet* alone, we learn something about what being a ghost is like. Once again, Shakespeare has laid a false trail in the first scene, by flattering the Elizabethan superstition that ghosts are spirits which 'usurp' the bodies of the dead, a Renaissance version of invading body-snatchers. When the ghost speaks, however, he is quick to confirm that he is indeed his father's spirit, 'doomed for a certain term to walk the night'. Later on, the ghost confirms that he is condemned to purgatory because of the manner of his death, 'cut off even in the blossoms of my sin... with all my imperfections on my head'.

Old Hamlet's Ghost cannot rest then, until his earthly account is settled by the avenging of his death. He lives in a terrible limbo; Hamlet's response to his first words is not horror but pity: 'Alas, poor ghost!' He is in that condition of ghostliness, of being between life and death, described by the Gravedigger's Boy's Ghost in the speech in which he asks Lear to let him stay:

> Let me stay with you, Lear. When I died, I went
> somewhere. I don't know where it was. I waited and
> nothing happened. And then I started to rot, like a body
> in the ground. Look at my hands, they're like an old

man's. They're withered. I'm young, but my stomach's
shrivelled up and the hair's turned white. Look, my arms!
Feel how thin I am. Are you afraid to touch me?

Old Hamlet's Ghost and the Gravedigger's Boy's Ghost are in
the same place. It is a place which Shakespeare's Lear inhabits
for most of the second half of the play. It is the place where the
most significant things in Shakespeare happen. We are led or
driven there by many agents; sometimes human, but often, too,
by witches, fairies, sprites and phantoms. It's the site of love
and death, of disrupted ceremony, of things made strange. It's
the liminal zone.

1. Michelene Wandor, *The Art of Writing Drama*, London: Methuen, 2008, pp. 126-7.

2. Steve Gooch, *Writing a Play*, London: A&C Black, 2001, pp. 98-9.

3. David Lodge, 'Pinter's *Last to Go*: A Structuralist Reading', in *The Practice of Writing*, London: Secker & Warburg, 1996, p. 275.

4. Keir Elam, *The Semiotics of Theatre and Drama*, London: Methuen, 1980, pp. 162-3.

5. Quoted in J.L. Styan, *The Elements of Drama*, Cambridge: Cambridge University Press, 1963, p. 12.

6. Quoted in *The Independent*, 6 February 1994.

7. Quoted in *The Guardian*, 30 May 1998.

8. Steven Rose, *The Making of Memory*, London: Vintage, 2003, p. 118.

9. Antony Sher, *Year of the King*, London: Chatto and Windus, reprinted by Nick Hern Books, London, 2004, p. 177.

10. Wandor, *op. cit.*, p. 135.

11. George Bernard Shaw, 'The Quintessence of Ibsenism', in *Major Critical Essays* (ed. Michael Holroyd), London and New York: Penguin, 1986, pp. 103-4.

12. Currently available as Thomas L. Berger, William C. Bradford and Sidney L. Sondergard, *An Index of Characters in Early Modern English Drama Printed Plays, 1500-1660*, Cambridge: Cambridge University Press, 1998.

8
Endings

Endings

I began with the idea that drama concentrated the chaos of life, removing its profuse redundancy, and exposing its underlying synchronicities, rhythms and shapes. I suggested that, in looking for connections between the apparently distinct, drama was reflecting the fundamental mechanisms of the human mind.

Discussing whole plays, I distinguished between story and plot. I noted how characters rebelled against the constraints placed upon them by a particular plot, and how plots themselves rebelled against the constraints of genre. I noted that, far from being a mechanical storytelling convenience, structure communicated meaning as deliberately as plotting, character or theme. Then I discussed the building blocks of plays: how scenes work, particularly when activated by the use of recognisable ceremonies drawn from the social world. Then I showed how devices – smaller mechanisms, within scenes or between them – manipulated time and space in order to draw attention to common patterns. Throughout, I've called that common pattern an 'action'.

That pattern – sometimes a 'despite' clause linked to another by the word 'nonetheless', more often a project followed by a reversal – can be detected at every level of the art. Plays have actions, but so do scenes. The action of a scene is often emplotted through a social format whose predictable course is disrupted by a reversal. This disruption is often brought about by characters who are unable or unwilling to perform the function required of them by their office or their rank.

Smaller ceremonies can function in the same way within scenes, as characters manipulate, subvert or abandon the sober project of drawing up to-do lists, preparing CVs or conducting roll-calls.

Such formats can do service as part of a compositional repertoire, being invested with related or analogous meaning, reappearing in different guises, revealing unexpected congruence or difference. Like lines, character traits, plotting points and metaphors, formats can become codes, whose repetition, manipulation and upending communicate meaning.

Plays themselves work within recognisable and predictable structures and patterns, providing expectations which the audience brings with them into the playhouse, whether we like it or not. A genre is a theatrical format. Romantic comedy is to *She Stoops to Conquer* what performance is to the first scene of *The Seagull*. Revenge tragedy is to the whole of *Hamlet* what funerals are to the graveyard scene. Like a format in a scene, a play's genre can be disrupted by the refusal of its characters to accept the requirements of their roles. Like its action – *as* its action – a play's genre contains a project (that virtue will be rewarded, villainy thwarted, Jack will get his Jill) which can be undermined, twisted or reversed.

Finally, plays both contain ceremonies and are ceremonies. Many of the most powerful ceremonies in plays take place in those strange places where we go to learn to love or to die. Such scenes are particularly powerful because the characters are doing in the play what we are doing at the play. Drama is about ceremonies and liminal zones; it *is* such a ceremony and such a zone. As religion turns the literally enacted rites of sacrifice into symbolic rituals, so the playwright takes the most agonising, painful, inspiring and deadly moments of human life and turns them into drama. Drama is a zone in which we can experiment with our dreams and our dreads, our ambitions and our impulses – murderous as well as virtuous – in conditions of safety. If the point of figurative painting is that it represents three dimensions on a flat plane, then the point of drama is that it's all pretend.

Now is a good time to repeat this. The profusion of narrative forms, the overlap of fact and fiction and the rise of interactive storytelling have allowed great confusion to arise about the very nature of fiction. A new censoriousness is abroad, based not on the state's desire to guard the public from corrupting influence, but on the public's insistence that it be protected from offence (whether that offence arises from the representation of distressing acts, like paedophilia, or of sacred objects, rituals or personages). The first form is based on the idea that to represent is to encourage, the second on the notion that to dramatise is to condone the wicked or belittle the virtuous.

Behind all of this is the idea that there are subjects too important, too profound, too dangerous for literature and drama to touch, that fiction-making is a trivial pursuit, a luxury pastime which, if it proves to be dangerous to its consumers, should be suppressed for the greater good, like high-risk sports, keeping attack dogs, or eating meat off the bone. We have been intimidated by such accusations – aided and abetted as they have been by postmodern critics in the universities – into ignoring or devaluing the positive role of storytelling in our lives. A proper concern with the lies and distortions which are presented to us as 'stories' should not blind us to the fact that storytelling is central to our being as humans. Without it, we would be constrained within the dungeon of our own direct experience. We would find it hard to plan – to imagine a series of actions and their consequences. And we couldn't empathise, with the good or with the bad.

The point of writing about the extremes of human behaviour is not to discourage wickedness by pointing out the inevitability of its comeuppance; 'Don't do this at home' is as misleading a description of what writing counsels as 'Go thou and do likewise'. The awful truth is that the response most great writing about wickedness provokes in us is neither 'Yes please' nor 'No thanks', but 'You too?' *Richard III* celebrates, nay, glorifies activities – brother-drowning, nephew-smothering, tyranny-imposing – that have no redeeming social value at all. True, he gets his just deserts. But what the first half of the play does is to confront us with the fact that this appalling man is the most vivid, thrilling and inspiring person onstage. Eric Bentley points out that while tragedy does not reflect the audience's actions (they have not committed murder), it 'reflects their souls, and in their souls they *have* committed murder'.[1] By enabling us to imagine what it is like to see the world through other eyes (including through the eyes of the violent and the murderous), drama develops capacities without which we cannot live together in societies at all.

The other thing I started with was a kind of apology. By trying to categorise the mechanisms of stage drama, wasn't I diminishing the complexity, the depth and the uniqueness of those great plays to which, surely, such rules don't apply? In 'The Quintessence of Ibsenism', Shaw said that what made Shakespeare great was what he has in common with Ibsen (argument), not what he has in common with Webster (melodrama).[2] But, in fact, Shakespeare is better than Webster not because of what he subtracted from the great Jacobean but because of what he added. Great plays aren't ordinary plays minus their limitations, but ordinary plays plus something else.

Part of that something else consists in originality and surprise. Another way of putting most of what I've argued in this book is to say that drama is about the balance between the expected (project, format, genre) and the surprising (reversal, disruption, twist). Without any surprise, a play becomes boring and predictable; but a play which consists entirely of surprise would be incomprehensible. Perhaps surprise is the wrong word here: having seen a British avant-garde play, Václav Havel realised 'with particular clarity' that 'nothing is quite so mutually exclusive in theatre as caprice and surprise'.[3]

On the other hand, when asked what were the two essentials of a great act, the Chief Executive of the Barnum and Bailey Circus answered: 'You get the audience to ask, "How did they do that?"' and you 'deliver the unexpected'. In that, the circus is following Aristotle, who argued that drama is 'heightened when things happen unexpectedly as well as logically, for then they will be more remarkable than if they seem merely mechanical or accidental'.[4] In saying this, Aristotle also anticipates Brecht and the Russian formalists, who believed the purpose of art was to make the familiar strange.

Nowhere is the balance between the surprising and the predictable, the familiar and strange, the conventional and the novel, more obvious than in the openings and endings of plays. By upending our notion of how plays should start and finish, playwrights acknowledge both that there are legitimate formal expectations, but that they have the right – cussedly – to defy them.

Hence, the remarkable number of plays referred to in this book which end with the word 'beginning': from Brecht's *The Life of Galileo* via Arnold Wesker's *Roots* to Charlotte Keatley's *My Mother Said I Never Should*. Hence, too, the use of a complementary device at the beginning of two plays which – you could say – bookend the 2,500 years of drama that we know about.

In Tony Harrison's translation, the first line of Aeschylus's *Oresteia* is 'No end to it all.' The first line of Samuel Beckett's *Endgame* is 'Finished. It's finished.'

Which, now, it is.

1. Eric Bentley, *The Life of the Drama*, London: Methuen, 1965, p. 304.

2. George Bernard Shaw, 'The Quintessence of Ibsenism', in *Major Critical Essays* (ed. Michael Holroyd), London and New York: Penguin, 1986, p. 167.

3   Václav Havel, *Letters to Olga*, London: Faber and Faber, 1990, p. 258.

4. Aristotle, 'Poetics' in *Classical Literary Criticism*, trans. T.S. Dorsch, London and New York: Penguin, 1965, p. 45.

Index

Note: Plays are dated by first appearance (publication or production). Because of the difficulties of dating pre-Commonwealth plays, dates are not given for plays written before 1642.